Rediscovering the True Meaning of Christmas

*A Collection of
Incarnation Sermons*

Rediscovering the True Meaning of Christmas

A Collection of Incarnation Sermons

P. G. Mathew

GRACE & GLORY MINISTRIES
Davis, California

ISBN: 978-0-9771149-4-8
Library of Congress Control Number: 2017958216

All scripture quotations, unless otherwise indicated, are taken from the 1984 version of the Holy Bible, New International Version®, NIV®. Copyright ©1973, 1978, 1984, 2011 by Biblica, Inc.™ Used by permission of Zondervan. All rights reserved worldwide. www.zondervan.com [Occasionally wording has been modified without notation to reflect author's preference and emphasis.]

The "NIV" and "New International Version" are trademarks registered in the United States Patent and Trademark Office by Biblica, Inc.™

Contents

About the Author

The Reverend P. G. Mathew, who holds three graduate degrees in theology from Central and Westminster theological seminaries (USA), is the founder and senior minister of Grace Valley Christian Center in California. Originally a scientist from India, he is also a former professor of Greek and systematic theology and has traveled widely for Christian mission interests. He is the author of *The Normal Church Life* (1 John); *Victory in Jesus* (Joshua); *The Wisdom of Jesus* (the Sermon on the Mount); *Muscular Christianity* (Hebrews); *The Joy of Christian Giving*; *The Gospel Freedom* (Romans 1–8); *The Gospel Life* (Romans 9–16); *Power of the Holy Spirit* (Acts); *Daily Delight* (devotional); *James: Fruitful Christian Faith* (James); and several other books, including commentaries on Isaiah and Matthew. He is also the founder and president of Grace Valley Christian Academy and Grace and Glory Foundation. For more information, visit *www.gracevalley.org*.

Introduction

What is the true meaning of Christmas? The Christmas of nostalgia and commercial sales is *not* the true Christmas message.

From the Bible, we learn that Christmas is the greatest event in human history. The eternal Son of God became man, born of the virgin Mary in a stable in the town of Bethlehem two thousand years ago. Jesus Christ lived a sinless life, yet was unjustly condemned to die on the cross of Calvary for our sins. We would never know the significance of these historical events without the revelation of the Bible. There is no gospel and no hope for mankind without Christmas.

Christmas is God's solution to man's root problem—the problem of sin. Joseph and Mary were told to give their baby the name Jesus, for he would save his people from their sins (Matt. 1:21). Jesus alone accomplished this salvation on behalf of his people by suffering the death penalty due to them for their sins in their place. This is substitutionary atonement (Isa. 53). The Bible says, "He was delivered over to death for our sins and was raised to life for our justification" (Rom. 4:25).

Jesus Christ is God's indescribable gift to sinners. "God so loved the world that he gave his one and only Son, that whoever believes in him shall not perish but have eternal life" (John 3:16).

The Lord Jesus Christ must be understood and embraced by faith if sinners would be saved. That is why this collection of sermons is highly relevant for us to read and understand. I am not advocating a return to the Christmas of nostalgia; rather, I am advocating a return to the Jesus of the Bible. This Jesus, "being the eternal Son of God, became man, and so was, and continues to be, God and man in two distinct natures, and one person, forever." He is the only Redeemer of God's elect.[1]

---

1   See the Westminster Shorter Catechism, Question 21.

This is a collection of Christmas sermons preached from 1996 to 2016. The incarnation of Christ was prophesied in the Old Testament, and all four of the gospel writers speak of it; thus, we have arranged these sermons in biblical order. In all of them, the unchanging gospel message rings clear: The infant Jesus, born in a stable to the virgin Mary, the baby whose birth we celebrate on Christmas day, is none other than Christ the Lord, the King of kings, the Creator and only Savior of the world.

I wish to thank my wife, Gladys; Mr. Marc Roby, Mr. Gregory Perry, Dr. Lisa Case, Mrs. Margaret Killeen, editing; Mr. Michael Ishii and Mrs. Christy Farris, formatting; Mrs. Jessica Contreras, cover design; and Mr. Daniel Washabaugh, production. *Soli Deo Gloria!*

P. G. Mathew

1
To Us a Son Is Given
ISAIAH 9:1–7

⁶For to us a child is born, to us a son is given, and the government will be on his shoulders. And he will be called Wonderful Counselor, Mighty God, Everlasting Father, Prince of Peace. ⁷Of the increase of his government and peace there will be no end. He will reign on David's throne and over his kingdom, establishing and upholding it with justice and righteousness from that time on and forever. The zeal of the LORD Almighty will accomplish this.

Isaiah 9:6–7

The first five verses of Isaiah 9 speak about the great joy of a group of people who had been sitting in darkness but who have now seen a great light. By a miracle, the yoke of these slaves was broken, the bar shattered, and they have begun to celebrate their great salvation with inexpressible joy. What is the reason for this great joy and celebration? *"For to us a child is born, to us a son is given"* (v. 6). In the Hebrew text it reads, *"Because a child is born to us, a son is given to us."* The emphasis is placed upon the child, the son, which speaks about the human and divine nature of Jesus Christ. This Jesus is the cause of our joy.

During a recent Christmas celebration in a large church, the senior pastor declared that his church is a fun church, where people can "hang with Jesus for fun." Additionally, he said, his church has no rules. This pastor is very clever. No doubt he observed that what most people want is fun, not rules.

We make no such declarations in this church, but we do say that a person can learn how to be truly happy by serving Jesus. Here we proclaim Jesus, who leads his people in the way of righteousness. Christianity is not lawlessness; rather, Christians delight in God's law, knowing it is the law of liberty. For a Christian, the yoke of Jesus is easy. The kingdom of God that we proclaim is "righteousness, peace and joy in the Holy Spirit" (Rom. 14:17). The apostle John tells us, "This is love for God: to obey his commands. And his commands are not burdensome" (1 John 5:3). Jesus said, "If you love me, you will obey what I command" (John 14:15). True joy comes from serving Jesus.

Who Is This Child?

At Christmas, we celebrate the birth of Jesus Christ—the promised Seed of the woman (Gen. 3:15), the seed of Abraham, of the tribe of Judah, the Son of David. We celebrate the birth of the son born in Bethlehem to the virgin Mary. We celebrate the birth of the Son of God.

Jesus once asked his disciples, "Who do you say that I am?" So we also must ask, "What sort of a man is Jesus Christ?" The gospels teach us that he is the one who commanded, and the wind and the waves obeyed; he is the one who healed the sick, cleansed lepers, raised the dead, and walked on water; and he is the one who taught with authority and prophesied that he would be raised from the dead.

The Mission of Jesus Christ

We must not see Jesus Christ, then, merely as a helpless infant lying in a manger in Bethlehem, but in the entirety of his mission. Paul writes, "But when the time had fully come, God sent his Son, born of a woman, born under law, to redeem those under law, that we might receive the full rights of sons" (Gal. 4:4–5).

The mission of Jesus Christ was to crush the head of the serpent and declare war upon all who are wicked. As the ever-victorious warrior, he did not come to give us fun or to usher in an age of antinomianism; he came to fulfill the law and destroy death itself.

This Jesus does not need our sympathy, lullabies, or material gifts. The Bible says that he who was rich became poor that we might become rich through his poverty (2 Cor. 8:9). Remember what he said to the women who were weeping for him on the day of his crucifixion: "Daughters of Jerusalem, do not weep for me; weep for yourselves and for your children" (Luke 23:28).

What is God's message to us at Christmas? "Don't feel sorry for Jesus as if he were a mere helpless infant. You must repent of your sins and trust in Christ alone for your salvation. Away with all sympathy and silly sentimentalism!"

God Becomes Man

Who, then, is this infant whose birth we celebrate at Christmas? First, he is God/man. As the late professor John Murray of Westminster Theological Seminary said, the incarnation of Christ is "the conjunction in one person of all that belongs to Godhead and all that belongs to manhood." "Incarnation" means "in flesh"; in the incarnation of Christ, God came and clothed himself in flesh. "The invisible became visible."[1] So Paul writes, "[Jesus] appeared in the flesh" (1 Tim. 3:16). John also writes of this, saying, "In the beginning was the Word, and the Word was with God, and the Word was God. . . . The Word became flesh and made his dwelling among us" (John 1:1, 14). That is why this One does not want our sympathy. He sympathizes with us, not the other way around.

God himself, the Word, became flesh and dwelt among us. The Son of God came in the likeness of man, yet he was without sin. Listen to this profound statement of Paul: "For what the law was powerless to do in that it was weakened by the sinful nature, God did by sending his own Son in the likeness of sinful man to be a sin offering" (Rom. 8:3).

Seven hundred years before the birth of Jesus Christ, Isaiah prophesied, "Therefore the Lord himself will give you a sign: Behold, the virgin will be with child and will give birth to a son, and will call him Immanuel" (Isa. 7:14). *Immanu* means "with us," and *El* means "God." This promised child would be the "with-us God." Just as God was with Israel in the wilderness to help them, so also Jesus Christ is God-with-us to save us, guide us, protect us,

---

1   John Murray, *Collected Writings*, vol. 2, *Systematic Theology* (Edinburgh: Banner of Truth, 1977), 133.

and provide for us. Because God is with us in Jesus Christ, we can always be triumphant and rejoice. We can do all things through Christ. We can resist temptation and cause the devil to flee. In Christ, we have all that we need. We can rejoice in tribulations and be fearless in the face of death.

John writes, "From the fullness of his grace we have all received one blessing after another" (John 1:16). Paul writes, "For God was pleased to have all his fullness dwell in him. . . . For in Christ all the fullness of the Deity lives in bodily form" (Col. 1:19; 2:9). God does not need anything from us, but we need everything from this God-with-us.

In Isaiah 6, we find a description of the glory of Christ before his incarnation:

> In the year that King Uzziah died, I saw the LORD seated on a throne, high and exalted, and the train of his robe filled the temple. Above him were seraphs, each with six wings: With two wings they covered their faces, with two they covered their feet, and with two they were flying. And they were calling to one another: "Holy, holy, holy is the LORD Almighty; the whole earth is full of his glory." At the sound of their voices the doorposts and thresholds shook and the temple was filled with smoke. (Isa. 6:1–4)

John 12:41 tells us that Isaiah was speaking in this passage about the second Person of the Trinity, the Lord Jesus Christ. The holy God of Isaiah 6 is Christ our Lord.

The Reason for Joy

As noted earlier, in Isaiah 9 we see a group of people rejoicing before the Lord. Why are they rejoicing? *"For to us a child is born"* (v. 6). "To us" means "for us, for our benefit, for our advantage, for our help." But in the Hebrew text the emphasis is not on "for us," but on "child." A child is born for us. This speaks about the human nature of Jesus Christ. Then we read, *"a son is given to us."* This emphasizes the divine nature of Christ. God so loved the world that he gave his only begotten Son (John 3:16).

Isaiah also says, *"The people walking in darkness have seen a great light"* (v. 2). They formerly were slaves, but now their yoke was broken, the bar across their shoulders was shattered, and the rod of their oppressors was destroyed. How did this happen? *"For to us a child is born, to us a son is given."*

The reason for our joyous celebration is found in the child, the second Person of the Trinity incarnate. There is no other explanation and no other Savior. This child, who was born of a virgin, without a human father, by the agency and power of the Holy Spirit, was born for us. And Luke 1:31 and Matthew 1:21 tell us that this child was to be named Jesus because he would save his people from their sins. This Jesus is *for us*—for our benefit, for our salvation. He saves, not everyone, but only his people, the elect of God.

When Jesus was born, the angel told the shepherds, "I bring good news to you." In the Greek, "to you" is in the dative of advantage. In other words, the good news is for the benefit of people like the poor shepherds, like Simeon, Anna, and Zechariah, and like us. The angel continued, "Today in the city of David is born to you a Savior." Then the heavenly host sang, "Glory to God in the highest, and on earth, peace to men of his good pleasure, upon whom God's good pleasure rests" (see Luke 2:10–14). Thus, this child was born, this son was given, for the salvation and joy of his people.

Wonderful Counselor

We are told this child *"will be called Wonderful Counselor"* (v. 6). The Hebrew text says, *"He is Wonder."* Jesus Christ is the greatest wonder imaginable because his very person is wonder: As God/man, there is no one else like him. In Judges 13, Samson's parents asked the angel, "What is your name?" The angel replied, "Why do you ask my name? It is wonderful." His name's incomprehensibility means he is God. Is Jesus a wonder to you? Have your eyes been opened to the person of Jesus Christ? He is wonder, especially to his people. He is Wonder of wonders.

Not only that, Jesus is also Counselor. In ancient times, kings, such as David, had counselors. Even today, our political leaders need counselors. But this One does not need any counselor. He is *the* Counselor and does all things according to the counsel of his own will. What he plans, he always fulfills. Paul writes, "Oh, the depth of the riches of the wisdom and knowledge of God!

How unsearchable his judgments, and his paths beyond tracing out! Who has known the mind of the Lord? Or who has been his counselor?" (Rom. 11:33–34).

God does not need our counsel, but we need his. Joshua failed to seek God's counsel and was deceived by the Gibeonites (Josh. 9). Saul, after being abandoned by God, sought the counsel of a witch (1 Sam. 28). The people of the world seek the counsel of mediums, spiritists, and "experts" who whisper and mutter nonsense: "When men tell you to consult mediums and spiritists, who whisper and mutter, should not a people inquire of their God?" (Isa. 8:19). But God has given us the counsel of his Son in the Bible.

Mighty God

Not only is this One the Wonderful Counselor, but he is also "Mighty God," (v. 6). In the Hebrew it is *El-Gibbor*, an expression that appears also in Isaiah 10:21. *El* means "God" and *Gibbor* means "warrior." Jesus Christ is God who is mighty in battle.

Consider what Jesus himself said: "I have told you these things, so that in me you may have peace. In this world you will have trouble. But take heart! I have overcome the world" (John 16:33). This God/man is Mighty God. Have you confessed him as such? Has he conquered you?

Everlasting Father

Jesus is also "Everlasting Father" (v. 6), or "Father of eternity." "Everlasting" points to his deity and "Father" to his humanity. Jesus is Father to us eternally. As our earthly fathers have cared for us, so also Christ cares for us, forgiving us, instructing us, providing for us, and loving us forever.

In Isaiah 63:16, God is called our Father: "But you are our Father, though Abraham does not know us or Israel acknowledge us; you, O LORD, are our Father, our Redeemer from of old is your name." And in Psalm 103:13 we read, "As a father has compassion on his children, so the LORD has compassion on those who fear him." Think about the father of the prodigal son, waiting for the sinner to return. He received him with great joy, saying, "Let us have a feast and celebrate, for this son of mine was dead and is alive again; he was lost and is found" (Luke 15:23–24). Jesus Christ is such a father to us.

Prince of Peace

This One is also called the "*Prince of Peace*" (v. 6). He is the prince who brings peace, not by negotiation, but by conquering all his enemies. Peace comes to us from the cross of Jesus Christ. Elsewhere Isaiah says, "The punishment that brought us peace was upon him, and by his wounds we are healed" (Isa. 53:5).

Because Christ died for our sins, he now can offer us peace. God's enemies are reconciled to him through the death of his own Son, as Paul writes: "Therefore, since we have been justified through faith, we have peace with God through our Lord Jesus Christ" (Rom. 5:1). God says of man, "'I have seen his ways, but I will heal him; I will guide him and restore comfort to him, creating praise on the lips of the mourners in Israel. Peace, peace, to those far and near,' says the LORD. 'And I will heal them'" (Isa. 57:18–19).

In Isaiah 66:12, God tells us, "I will extend peace to her like a river." I cannot understand how Christians can sit in gloom and misery, complaining and murmuring. But if you find yourself in this condition, I hope you will look at this promise from the Prince of Peace. God promises to give us his peace in abundance. Jesus told his disciples, "Peace I leave with you; my peace I give you. I do not give to you as the world gives. Do not let your hearts be troubled and do not be afraid" (John 14:27).

The world cannot give us peace. Pax Romana came and went. Now Pax Americana has come and is going. But the Prince of Peace says he will extend everlasting peace to us like a river. That is why the heavenly host could sing at the first Christmas, "Glory to God in the highest, and on earth peace to men on whom his favor rests."

Peace and Government

Peace means salvation in its fullness. This child accomplished it by his life and by his death on the cross. Isaiah says, "*Of the increase of his government and peace there will be no end*" (v. 7). There is a link between having God's government in your life and experiencing peace. If someone tells you, "Come to our church for fun; we don't have any rules," that person does not understand this linkage. Where God's government is, there will be peace. So if you want more peace, you must come under greater government.

Remember the condition of the people before this Son came to them? They were blind, sitting in darkness, and cursing God (Isa. 8:19–22). This describes the life of any who are outside of God, who refuse to consult the word of God and be guided by his truth.

But Isaiah tells us that God was going to save a certain people, called "his people," for whom there would be no more gloom: *"Nevertheless, there will be no more gloom for those who were in distress. In the past he humbled the land of Zebulun and the land of Naphtali, but in the future he will honor Galilee of the Gentiles, by the way of the sea, along the Jordan"* (v. 1). This was literally fulfilled when Jesus Christ grew up and ministered in that part of the world, where many people were able to come hear him and be healed and saved by him.

Jesus Christ Is King

We have said that this child promised by Isaiah is God. But not only is he God, he is also King—the everlasting, final King. There is no king after him in the house of David. He is the royal Son of David as well as David's Lord.

So Isaiah declares, *"Of the increase of his government and peace there will be no end. He will reign on David's throne and over his kingdom, establishing and upholding it with justice and righteousness from that time on and forever. The zeal of the LORD Almighty will accomplish this"* (v. 7).

The eternality of Christ's kingdom was emphasized when God first announced the Davidic covenant: "He is the one who will build a house for my Name, and I will establish the throne of his kingdom forever" (2 Sam. 7:13). If we read the history of Judah, however, we see that there was no king in the house of David who ruled forever. In fact, after the fall of Jerusalem, the kingdom fell apart and the people became slaves of foreign powers, as Nehemiah prayed: "We are slaves today, slaves in the land you gave our forefathers" (Neh. 9:36). Nevertheless, God would keep the promise made to David concerning his son:

> I will establish the throne of his kingdom forever. I will be his father, and he will be my son. When he does wrong, I will punish him with the rod of men, with floggings inflicted by men. But my love will never be taken away from him, as I took it away from Saul, whom I removed from before you. Your house and your kingdom will endure forever before me; your throne will be established forever. (2 Sam. 7:13–16)

David's throne is eternal, and, in God's time, the promise was fulfilled. The virgin conceived by the power of the Holy Spirit and gave birth to a son, Jesus Christ.

When the angel Gabriel appeared to Mary in Nazareth, he referred to this promise as well as to what God had spoken through Isaiah concerning the kingship of the Messiah (Isa. 9). So in Luke 1:32–33 we read, "He will be great and will be called the Son of the Most High. The Lord God will give him the throne of his father David, and he will reign over the house of Jacob forever; his kingdom will never end." Jesus Christ is the final and everlasting King of his kingdom. He has a people whom he will rule.

Here again we see the foolishness of a church having no rules. If we truly understand Jesus Christ, we will never speak about "hanging with him for fun." He demands that we worship him as God and serve him as King.

We can never escape Jesus Christ as God and King. His government will always increase. Jesus himself taught us to pray, "Thy kingdom come, thy will be done, on earth as it is in heaven" (Matt. 6:10, KJV). We see God's government displayed in the actions of the angel Gabriel. At the command of God, he went to Nazareth, entered Mary's house, and greeted her. This is the way the angels operate. They always render complete, joyful, and immediate obedience to their great King. This King destroys all other kingdoms. He alone rules in justice and righteousness to the ends of the earth, and his kingdom is forever.

Why are people miserable, fearful, anxious and confused? They are not under the rule of King Jesus. We read, "There is no peace for the wicked" (Isa. 48:22). Jesus told the false Christians, "Depart from me, you workers of iniquity!" (Matt. 7:23). The notion that we can negate Christ as King and yet have peace is false. If we want true peace, we first must submit to the government of God in our lives.

There is no end to the increase of the government of Jesus Christ; no one can successfully oppose him at his second coming. Christ's first coming was in humiliation, but his second coming will be in great manifest glory.

What about those who rebel against God? The Bible tells us that rebellion is like witchcraft (1 Sam. 15:23). Where there is rebellion, there is demon activity. But no one can oppose God successfully. He is King of kings and Lord of lords. He is the one of whom the wise men asked, "Where is the one who has been born king of the Jews?" (Matt. 2:2).

He is King, not only of the Jews, but also of the Gentiles. He is the King of everyone. Every person of every other religion, and even atheists, must surrender to him. If this is true, why are some people still stubborn? It means they have not understood who this God and King is.

But, rejoice, church, in God's great power, wisdom, and rule, because his kingship benefits us. A son is born, a child is given for us, for our advantage and benefit. Yes, he will destroy all who refuse to surrender to him, but he will also save all who confess, "Jesus is Lord."

God wants us to worship and serve him. When Saul of Tarsus was arrested by this King on the road to Damascus, the first question he asked was, "Who are you, Lord?" The answer came, "I am Jesus of Nazareth, whom you persecute." Then Paul asked, "What do you want me to do, O Lord?" And he confessed many years later, "I have not been disobedient to the heavenly vision of the glory of the resurrected Christ" (see Acts 26:19).

Jesus Christ is King, and no one will be saved without confessing that he is Lord.

Jesus Christ Is Savior

Not only is Jesus our God and King, but he is also our Savior. That is why in Isaiah 9:1–5 the people are rejoicing. This child, this son, will save his people and give joy to those who once lived in darkness and were under the tyranny of Satan.

"His name is Jesus, for he will save his people from their sins" (see Matt. 1:21). What does the Bible mean when it says that God will save us from our sins? First, we must recognize that there is such a thing as sin, and that we are sinners by nature. We are so used to our sin that we do not even recognize it. Remember the lame man of Acts 3? This man was accustomed to his affliction. He heard about Jesus, but what did he ask Peter for? He asked not for healing but for a little money. We also are seriously crippled by sin, but what do we want? As long as we have a little money, we are happy. But Jesus Christ saves us from sin: first, from its guilt; second, from its pollution, which permeates our entire being; third, from its power; and fourth, from its punishment.

Not only does Jesus save us from something, but he also saves us for something. He saves us for glory. He saves us for blessing. He saves us for fellowship with God. He saves us for eternal life. He saves us for eternal pleasures. The psalmist says, "In thy presence is fullness of joy; at thy right hand there are pleasures for evermore" (Ps. 16:11, KJV). Jesus saves us so we can be adopted as sons and made heirs of God and joint heirs with Christ. He saves us so we can have authority and rule with him.

How does he save us? By his life and death. He came, not to be ministered unto, but to minister and to give his life as a ransom for many. We needed a God/man to save us, and Hebrews 2 tells us that we have such a qualified mediator in Jesus Christ. He who is perfect God and perfect man died on the cross for our sins and was raised for our justification.

Jesus Christ is God, King, and Savior of the world. The Samaritan people recognized this and told him, "You are the Savior of the world" (John 4:42). Peter declared in Acts 4:12, "Salvation is found in no one else."

In Genesis 3, God first promised to send a Savior; in Isaiah's prophecy, that promise was repeated with the additional disclosure that the Savior would be a virgin-born Son who would also be Mighty God. This promise was fulfilled seven hundred years after Isaiah's prediction when the virgin Mary became pregnant, not by a man, but by divine action, and brought forth a son, Jesus Christ.

So we read, *"To us a child is born, to us a son is given"* (v. 6). Who is this child? He is God. He is the King eternal. He is the only Savior of the world. The angel said, "I bring you good news of great joy. . . . Today in the town of David a Savior has been born to you; he is Christ the Lord" (Luke 2:10–11).

What about You?

Is Jesus Christ your God? Do you worship him? Is he your King? Have you surrendered to him and embraced his rule and laws? Is he your Savior? Have you trusted in him alone for your eternal salvation?

I hope you will not view Jesus as one who needs your sympathy. There are people who come to church once a year, every year, to celebrate Christmas. But even after a whole lifetime of celebrating Christmas, they die without Christ. Every Christmas is a great opportunity to surrender to this God, this King, this Savior. If you are included in those for whom this child is born, you will repent and believe on this God/man.

Is Jesus your God, King, and Savior? He has come to you; have you come to him? He says, "Come to me, all you who are weary and burdened, and I will give you rest" (Matt. 11:28). Have you seen the great light? Has your iron yoke of sin been broken and shattered by him? Have you experienced liberation from sin— from its guilt, pollution, power, and punishment?

If Jesus is your God, King, and Savior, then you have a God-given right to be happy. But if he is not, you are still in your sins. You are a slave to fear, and it is impossible for you to be happy. My counsel to you is to repent and believe on Jesus, the Savior of the world. Come to him and acknowledge him, saying, "You are God, and you are my God. You are King of kings and Lord of lords, and you are my King. Rule my life, that I may have peace," and, finally, "You are Savior of the world, and you are also my Savior."

May God deliver us from sentimentalism, stupidity, emptiness of mind, and silly conformity to the ideas of the world. May we be sober-minded and recognize that this child, this son, this divine gift whose birthday we celebrate at Christmas, is Mighty God, the great King and only Savior of the world. When we do so, we will be able to rejoice with joy unspeakable and full of glory, and our lives will be filled with peace because his rule is in our hearts.

2
The Shepherd of Israel

MICAH 5:1–5

¹Marshal your troops, O city of troops, for a siege is laid against us. They will strike Israel's ruler on the cheek with a rod. ²"But you, Bethlehem Ephrathah, though you are small among the clans of Judah, out of you will come for me one who will be ruler over Israel, whose origins are from of old, from ancient times." ³Therefore Israel will be abandoned until the time when she who is in labor gives birth and the rest of his brothers return to join the Israelites. ⁴He will stand and shepherd his flock in the strength of the LORD, in the majesty of the name of the LORD his God. And they will live securely, for then his greatness will reach to the ends of the earth. ⁵And he will be their peace.

Micah 5:1–5

A Word of Prophecy

The prophet Micah was a contemporary of Isaiah. Micah also spoke about the promised child, the coming Messiah. He spoke specifically about the place of his birth. Micah gave his prophecy about 700 BC.

Only the God of Israel is able to disclose the future accurately, and he does so through his prophets. God alone knows all things. He alone reveals the end from the beginning. Thus, all claims of idols to reveal the future are lies.

Because they knew Micah's prophecy, the chief priests and scribes were able to tell Herod exactly where the Messiah was to be born (Matt. 2:4–6). Even ordinary people knew that the Messiah was to be born in Bethlehem in the district of Ephrathah (John 7:42).

Tiny Bethlehem

Micah begins, *"But you, Bethlehem Ephrathah, though you are small among the clans of Judah, out of you will come for me one who will be ruler over Israel, whose origins are from old, from ancient times"* (v. 2). Micah was speaking of a tiny, insignificant town. "Bethlehem" means "house of bread." The Bible mentions two Bethlehems. One was located in the land of Zebulun in the north, seven miles northwest of Nazareth (Josh. 19:15). But this prophecy is not referring to the northern Bethlehem. Notice, *"But you, Bethlehem Ephrathah . . ."* This Bethlehem was located in the south, in Judea, in the district of Ephrathah, which means "fruitful." Six miles southwest of Jerusalem, it was the burial place of Rachel, Jacob's wife (Gen. 35:19). Later, Boaz and Ruth lived there, as did Jesse. God sent Samuel to Bethlehem to anoint one of Jesse's sons, a very unpromising shepherd boy named David. During David's early years, Bethlehem was occupied by the Philistines.

Bethlehem of Ephrathah in Judea was the least of the towns of Judah. In fact, it did not make the list of one hundred and fifteen prominent towns of Judah recorded in Joshua 15:20–63. Like Nazareth, Bethlehem was despised by people. It was excluded from the clans of Judah. It was small, it was insignificant, it was nothing.

But God has a way of exalting the despised. So Micah's prophecy speaks of the king of Israel, the Messiah, coming not out of Jerusalem but out of Bethlehem of Ephrathah. So we read, *"But you, Bethlehem Ephrathah, though you are small among the clans of Judah, out of you will come for me one who will be ruler over Israel"* (v. 2). God puts down the arrogant, exalts the humble, and comforts the weary.

Paul speaks about this principle of God exalting the despised things: "Brothers, think of what you were when you were called. Not many of you were wise by human standards; not many were influential; not many were of noble birth. But God chose the foolish things of the world to shame the wise; God chose the weak things of the world to shame the strong. He chose the lowly things of this world and the despised things—and the things that are not—to nullify the things that are, so that no one may boast before him" (1 Cor. 1:26–29).

Bethlehem was the birthplace of David, and it was to become the birthplace of David's Son and Lord. Later, in the fourth century, Helena, the mother of Emperor Constantine, erected a church over some caves in Bethlehem to memorialize the birthplace of Jesus. This church was later destroyed and then rebuilt by Justinian in the sixth century AD. The despised Bethlehem has now become world-famous. Multitudes of people follow the Magi to Bethlehem, where Jesus was born, and where many infants later were killed by Herod.

King of Israel

Micah's prophecy declares that the one to be born in Bethlehem would also be born the king of Israel. We read, *"Out of you will come for me one who will be ruler over Israel"* (v. 2). God's covenant people sinned and God chastised them severely by sending them into exile. Yet God's covenant with Abraham and David was not abrogated or invalidated. God is faithful, and God, unlike human beings, keeps his covenant. "God is not a man, that he should lie, nor a son of man, that he should change his mind" (Num. 23:16).

God articulated his covenant with David in 2 Samuel 7:16: "Your house and your kingdom will endure forever before me; your throne will be established forever." God promised that in due time a king, the Son of David, would come to rule Israel and the whole world. Micah 5:1 talks about a ruler being smitten on the cheek. That speaks about a failed, humiliated king. But that is not the end of the story. Another king would come—a victorious, conquering king.

Micah tells us that this coming king would be supernatural. Look at verse 2 again: *"Out of you will come for me one who will be ruler over Israel, whose origins are from of old, from ancient times,"* meaning from eternity. In other words, the prophet is saying, "This One is the eternal God" (see also Isa. 7:14; 9:6–7). Jesus told the Jews, "Before Abraham was born, I am!" (John 8:58). He is the Eternal One.

But not only is this king eternal, he is also human. We read, *"Therefore, Israel will be abandoned until the time when she who is in labor gives birth"* (v. 3). Micah is speaking about the coming of Jesus in the flesh. Until he came, Israel was abandoned—there were no kings in Israel from the exile of 586 BC until the birth of Christ.

In God's time, he sent his Son. The angel told Mary, "You will be with child and will give birth to a son, and you are to give him the name Jesus. He will be great and will be called the Son of the Most High. The Lord God will give him the throne of his father David, and he will reign over the house of Jacob forever; his kingdom will never end" (Luke 1:31–33).

This One would not only rule over the house of Jacob, but he would also be the king of the whole world. Micah declares, *"He will stand and shepherd his flock in the strength of the* LORD, *in the majesty of the name of the* LORD *his God. And they will live securely, for then his greatness will reach to the ends of the earth"* (v. 4). Jesus is coming to rule the whole world. He is God eternal, in human flesh. He is the king of Israel and the king of the world.

The Good Shepherd

Jesus is king, but he is also the shepherd of God's people. So Micah says, *"He will stand and shepherd his flock"* (v. 4). Unlike the shepherds of Ezekiel 34, who ate their sheep, this shepherd would feed his flock, heal his flock, search for his flock, find his flock, provide for his flock, and defend his flock. Beyond that, he would lay down his life for his flock, and he would do so voluntarily and vicariously. In John 10, Jesus said, "I am the good shepherd. The good shepherd lays down his life for the sheep. . . . My sheep know me—just as the Father knows me and I know the Father—and I lay down my life for the sheep. . . . The reason my Father loves me is that I lay down my life—only to take it up again. No one takes it from me, but I lay it down of my own accord. I have authority to lay it down and authority to take it up again" (John 10:11, 15, 17–18).

Paul tells us about the vicarious sacrifice of Jesus Christ in Romans 5:6–8: "You see, at just the right time, when we were still powerless, Christ died for [*huper*, that is, "in place of"] the ungodly. Very rarely will anyone die for a righteous man, though for a good man someone might possibly dare to die. But God demonstrates his own love for us in this: While we were still sinners, Christ died for [*huper*, in place of] us."

Jesus came to die in our place. As a result, his people are secure. So Micah says, *"And they will live securely"* (v. 4). Later, Jesus himself promised, "I give them eternal life, and they shall never perish; no one can snatch them out of my hand. My Father, who has given them to me, is greater than all; no one can snatch them out of my Father's hand. I and the Father are one" (John 10:28–29). This shepherd gives us eternal security.

David was a shepherd, and the Son of David would also be a shepherd. In ancient times, shepherds were looked down upon by others. They belonged to the lowest rung of society. They were seen as thieves and robbers. Rabbis forbade anyone from buying anything from a shepherd because they assumed the lowly shepherd would be selling stolen goods. And because of their low status, shepherds were not permitted to be witnesses in a court of law.

But as we said, God exalts the despised and lowly. So he announced the birth of the Shepherd-King, Jesus, not to the mighty and powerful of Jerusalem, but to the despised shepherds of lowly Bethlehem. They were the first to hear the good news of great joy and the first to go and worship the great Shepherd of the sheep. Those who could not witness in court became the first witnesses of the good news of Christ's birth.

Mary the mother of Jesus spoke about God putting down the arrogant and lifting up the despised. "[God] has performed mighty deeds with his arm; he has scattered those who are proud in their inmost thoughts. He has brought down rulers from their thrones but has lifted up the humble. He has filled the hungry with good things but has sent the rich away empty" (Luke 1:51–53). This is still true. Proud people will never believe in Jesus unless they forsake their pride. And those who are rich in this world will remain empty of eternal life unless they repent and believe. But this Shepherd-King will comfort the miserable, exalt the despised, and save the lost.

Prince of Peace

Finally, Micah says, *"And he will be their peace"* (v. 5). Jesus the Messiah is our peace, our shalom. Today our world has no peace. But this is nothing new. Since the Fall, as we read in Genesis 3, there is no peace for the wicked. The wrath of God abides on all sinners. They are naked, restless, and lost. They run away from the God who alone can save them. Instead they are trusting in their power and money to save them and give them peace.

What does it profit if you gain the whole world and lose your immortal soul? We cannot have peace with God until our sins are forgiven. But who can atone for our sins? All are sinners. That is why God sent his own Son, God/man, perfect man, sinless man, to live and die in our place and thus secure peace for us. Jesus is our peace. He alone can give us true peace with God.

How did Jesus establish this peace? Paul, perhaps reflecting on this particular verse, writes of Christ, "For he himself is our peace, who has made the two one and has destroyed the barrier, the dividing wall of hostility, by abolishing in his flesh the law with its commandments and regulations. His purpose was to create in himself one new man out of the two, thus making peace, and in this one body to reconcile both of them to God through the cross, by which he put to death their hostility. He came and preached peace to you who were far away and peace to those who were near" (Eph. 2:14–17). The apostle also says, "Having been justified by faith, we have peace with God" (Rom. 5:1).

There is no peace outside of one's relationship with Jesus Christ. He is peace. He alone is peace. He is my peace. Is he your peace? You may not experience another Christmas Eve, and I am asking you to consider: Do you have peace? If you die tonight, are you sure that you will go to the very presence of God because you trusted in Jesus Christ alone? He calls you to come to him and trust in him. He is peace, he is life, he is righteousness. He is resurrection, sanctification, and redemption. Believe on this Christ Child. Worship him alone for your peace.

All the gifts under the tree cannot save you. All the gods of the world cannot save you. They are all lies. You cannot save yourself; your children cannot save you. What about your grandchildren? They cannot save you either. Only this child of Bethlehem can save you—this child, wrapped in cloths and lying in a manger— he is the only one who can save you. He is God wrapped in human flesh.

So I offer you as your Savior the King Eternal, the Shepherd of Bethlehem, the crucified, risen Lord Jesus Christ, the Prince of peace. Kiss him, worship him, and praise him. He gives peace to his flock. As his flock, follow him, and you shall lack nothing.

3
The Genealogy of Jesus Christ

MATTHEW 1:1–17

A record of the genealogy of Jesus Christ the son of David, the son of Abraham.

Matthew 1:1

Have you ever systematically read through the Bible? If so, what did you do when you came to the first nine chapters of 1 Chronicles? If you are honest, you will probably say that you skipped these chapters, as most people do. Genealogy can be extremely boring, and, generally, we do not look forward with great delight to reading it. But in the gospels we find a genealogy that gives us great hope and encouragement. Why? The grand climax of this genealogy is God's Son, our Lord Jesus Christ, the Savior of the world and the King of all nations.

The genealogy of Jesus Christ is recorded in most of the gospel accounts. Matthew begins his gospel with these words: *"A record of the genealogy of Jesus Christ the son of David, the son of Abraham"* (v. 1). Matthew traces Christ's genealogy in a descending order from Abraham to Jesus. After telling of the events surrounding Christ's birth and the beginning of his public ministry, Luke traces Christ's genealogy in ascending order from Jesus to David to Abraham to Adam (Luke 3:23–38). Mark does not give a genealogy, but John traces the origin of our Lord to eternity. He says, "In the beginning was the Word, and the Word was with God, and the Word was God. . . . The Word became flesh and made his dwelling among us" (John 1:1, 14). And we must note that John's emphasis on eternity is in accordance with Micah's prophecy: "But you, Bethlehem Ephrathah, though you are small among the clans of Judah, out of you will come for me one who will be ruler over Israel, whose origins are from of old, from ancient times" (Mic. 5:2).

A Record of the Genealogy

In this study, we will consider the genealogy as found in Matthew 1:1–17. First, we must examine the title: "A *record of the genealogy of Jesus Christ*" (v. 1). This literally means, "*The book of the generation of Jesus Christ*," but there are questions about this title. It could be that this is the title to the genealogical list that we find in verses 2 through 17, or it may be a title or caption to the first two chapters of Matthew, which speak about the birth of Jesus Christ. According to some scholars, it could even mean the title to the entire gospel of Matthew.

We see this phrase "a record of the genealogy" or "the book of the generation" also in the Greek translation of the Old Testament called the Septuagint. In Genesis 5:1, we read, "This is the written account of Adam's line." In the same way, Matthew gives us a record of the genealogy of Jesus Christ, the last Adam, who will make all things new. Through Christ, there will be a new creation, a new man, a new heaven, and a new earth.

The Name of Jesus Christ

Matthew uses the name "*Jesus*," which is a shortened form of Jehoshua or Jeshua, meaning "the LORD saves." The emphasis in the name of Jesus is on the action he would perform, which is salvation of his people. The angel told Joseph, "You are to give him the name Jesus, because he will save his people from their sins" (Matt. 1:21).

Matthew also uses the word "*Christ*," which means the Messiah, the Spirit-anointed one. Jesus is the Christ, the one who has been qualified to do a task. What is that task? First, it is the task of revealing God, which is the task of a prophet. Second, it is the task of saving sinners, which is the task of a priest; Christ offered himself as the perfect and sufficient sacrifice for our sins. And third, it is the task of dominion, which is the task of a king. Jesus Christ is the King of kings and Lord of lords. He is the one who will rule and reign over all.

Jesus himself spoke about this anointing. In the synagogue at Nazareth he read from Isaiah 61, saying, "'The Spirit of the Lord is on me, because he has anointed me to preach good news to the poor. He has sent me to proclaim freedom for the prisoners and recovery of sight for the blind, to release the oppressed, to proclaim the year of the Lord's favor.' Then he rolled up the scroll, gave it back to the attendant and sat down. The eyes of everyone in the synagogue were fastened on him, and he began by saying to them, 'Today this scripture is fulfilled in your hearing'" (Luke 4:18–21).

Truly, Jesus is the Christ—the anointed Prophet, Priest, and King. Moses spoke about him as prophet: "The LORD your God will raise up for you a prophet like me from among your own brothers. You must listen to him" (Deut. 18:15). What would happen if someone did not listen? God himself said, "If anyone does not listen to my words that the prophet speaks in my name, I myself will call him to account" (Deut. 18:19). God will judge such a person. And in the New Testament, the Father said concerning Christ, "This is my Son, whom I love; with him I am well pleased. Listen to him!" (Matt. 17:5).

God's beloved Son, Jesus Christ, came as the Prophet to declare to us who God is and how we can be saved. He is also the Priest, anointed not after the order of Aaron, but a priest forever after the order of Melchizedek (Ps. 110). And not only that, Jesus Christ is also the King who rules with an iron scepter (Ps. 2).

Son of David

Matthew further identifies Jesus as *"the son of David"* (v. 1). Matthew was harking back to the Davidic covenant. God promised David that through his offspring the throne of his kingdom would be everlasting: "Your house and your kingdom will endure forever before me; your throne will be established forever" (2 Sam. 7:16).

Who is the seed of David through whom his kingdom would be established forever? The offspring God was referring to was not Solomon, but Jesus, declares Matthew. David was a great warrior who conquered all the enemies of Israel, but only for a season. But the kingship of Jesus, David's son, is forever. As King of kings, Jesus will conquer all his enemies and bring about eternal peace and salvation for his people.

Jesus is not only the Son of David, but he is also the Lord of David (Matt. 22:41–46). Isaiah spoke about him seven hundred years before his birth: "A shoot will come up from the stump of Jesse" (Isa. 11:1). The tree of the Davidic kingdom would be cut down, but a shoot, Jesus Christ, would come up, and we see this reflected in Matthew's genealogy. The genealogy is divided into three sections. The first section speaks about the rise of the Davidic kingdom, the second section speaks about its decline, and the third section speaks about its eclipse.

The tree of the Davidic kingdom was cut down and simply a stump was left. But Isaiah saw it and said, "A shoot will come up from the stump of Jesse; from his roots a Branch will bear fruit. The Spirit of the LORD will rest on him—the Spirit of wisdom and of understanding, the Spirit of counsel and of power, the Spirit of knowledge and of the fear of the LORD—and he will delight in the fear of the LORD" (Isa. 11:1–3). Isaiah also said, "For to us a child is born, to us a son is given, and the government will be on his shoulders. And he will be called Wonderful Counselor, Mighty God, Everlasting Father, Prince of Peace. Of the increase of his government and peace there will be no end. He will reign on David's throne and over his kingdom, establishing and upholding it with justice and righteousness from that time on and forever" (Isa. 9:6–7).

Jesus is this Branch, this child, this son. He is the Son of David, the King of kings and the Lord of lords, the One who will conquer all his enemies and bring about peace and salvation for his people.

Son of Abraham

Jesus is also *"the son of Abraham"* (v. 1). Matthew is referring to the Abrahamic covenant, which we find in Genesis 12:1–3: "The

LORD had said to Abram, 'Leave your country, your people and your father's household and go to the land I will show you. I will make you into a great nation and I will bless you; I will make your name great, and you will be a blessing. I will bless those who bless you, and whoever curses you I will curse; and all peoples on earth will be blessed through you.'" The Lord later told Abraham, "I will make you very fruitful; I will make nations of you, and kings will come from you. I will establish my covenant as an everlasting covenant between me and you and your descendants after you for the generations to come, to be your God and the God of your descendants after you" (Gen. 17:6–7). God also told Abraham that through his offspring "all nations on earth will be blessed" (Gen. 22:18). The blessing is not coming through Abraham but through his offspring. Who is Abraham's offspring? It is Jesus Christ. That is what Matthew has in mind.

When we examine the events surrounding the birth of Isaac, we must note that there was supernatural activity in the life of Abraham and Sarah in accordance with God's promise. And when you look at the events around the birth of Jesus, there was also supernatural activity. Both were supernatural events, but only Jesus was virgin-born. It is Jesus, not Isaac, who is the offspring of Abraham through whom all the families of the earth will be blessed. Paul clearly states, "The promises were spoken to Abraham and to his seed. The Scripture does not say 'and to seeds,' meaning many people, but 'and to your seed,' meaning one person, who is Christ" (Gal. 3:16). Beyond the shadow of doubt, Paul identifies the seed of Abraham, through whom all the nations of the earth will be blessed, as Jesus.

Son of Judah

Then Matthew says that Jesus is the seed of Judah: *"Judah, the father of Perez and Zerah, whose mother was Tamar"* (v. 3). Why is Judah in this genealogy? Why is it not Reuben, who was the oldest of Jacob's sons, or Simeon or Levi, who were older than Judah? Why is godly Joseph not listed here? The answer to all of these questions is divine election. God is sovereign, and he does what he pleases. Who can tell him what he should do or why? Who can thwart his purposes? Both Nebuchadnezzar and Job had to learn that. The sovereign Lord does what he pleases, and all that he does is just, true, and right.

We know something about Judah from the Genesis account. He was not an honorable character. He routinely committed adultery and engaged in prostitution. Then why is Judah listed here in the genealogy of God's holy Son? Again, God's choosing is according to his own sovereign will. As Paul says, "It does not, therefore, depend on man's desire or effort, but on God's mercy" (Rom. 9:16).

The Spirit of God came upon Jacob before he died and he prophesied about Judah. All his sons were with him, including Joseph, Reuben, Simeon, and Levi. But Jacob said, "The scepter," meaning rulership, "will not depart from Judah, nor the ruler's staff from between his feet, until he comes to whom it belongs and the obedience of the nations is his" (Gen. 49:10). From Judah came David, and from David came Jesus, the King of kings and the Lord of lords. This was divine determination, divine election, and divine good pleasure.

A List of Women

There are some particular abnormalities we notice in Matthew's genealogy. First, we see the names of five women in this list. Normally, Jewish genealogical lists did not contain the names of women because women were regarded as things, not persons. A woman was merely the possession of her father or husband to dispense with as he wished. In fact, in his regular morning prayers, a Jewish man of that time would thank God that he had not made him a Gentile, a slave, or a woman. So the inclusion of women's names in this genealogy is surprising. One woman is Mary, but who are the other four?

The first woman listed is Tamar. Tamar was a Gentile, a Canaanite, who played the role of a prostitute. She was the daughter-in-law of Judah, who fathered Perez and Zerah by her through prostitution. Yet her name and the name of one of her sons is in the genealogical record of the ancestry of Jesus. If we really think about that, we must be surprised and shocked.

The second woman is Rahab, another Gentile. She was probably the leading prostitute in the city of Jericho at the time. Yet she is also listed in this genealogy, and in Hebrews 11:31 we are told of her faith in God. Rahab believed God, was saved, and became the mother of Boaz, the ancestor of David and Jesus.

The third woman is Ruth, who was a foreigner, a Moabitess. God prohibited any Moabite or his descendants to enter the assembly of the Lord, even to the tenth generation (Deut. 23:3). Yet we find Ruth, a true believer, in this genealogy—Ruth, the wife of Boaz and mother of Obed.

The fourth woman is not named but she is described as Uriah's wife. We know her as Bathsheba, and she may have also been a Gentile, according to some scholars. One thing we do know is that Bathsheba was an adulteress who married David, who himself was a murderer, adulterer, and thief. Yet in the divine plan, Bathsheba is included in the genealogy of the Holy One, Jesus.

The inclusion of Tamar, Rahab, Ruth, and Bathsheba tells us that Christ breaks down all barriers of race, whether Jew or Gentile. He breaks down all distinctions of sex, whether male or female, and any other distinctions, whether righteous or unrighteous, saint or sinner. Truly, in Jesus Christ, the seed of Abraham, will all the peoples of the earth be blessed. It reminds us that God is no respecter of persons, but he shows mercy to whomever he desires to show mercy. The inclusion of the names of these women should give us great hope. The Bible says, "*Whosoever* believes on him shall not perish but have everlasting life" (John 3:16). And as Paul writes in Romans 3:22–23, "There is no difference, for all have sinned and fall short of the glory of God." All must be saved, and Jesus will not discriminate. The Savior will receive all people who will come to him in faith.

A List of Sinners

The inclusion of men should give us great hope too, for these men were sinners also. Look at Abraham. He lied several times and was not very considerate of his wife. In fact, he was timid and self-protective. Look at Isaac. He lied for his own benefit and also put his wife's life in jeopardy to protect himself. Look at Jacob. He was a cheat and a schemer. Look at Judah. He was an immoral person. Look at David. He was a lustful, scheming murderer and adulterer. God chose all of these and included them in this genealogy as well as in his book of life.

There is no one righteous; all have sinned (Rom. 3:10, 23). Therefore, let us be encouraged by this genealogical list. It tells us that God shows mercy in his Son to Gentiles, to Jews, to sinners, and to outcasts. His name truly is Jesus "because he will save his people from their sins."

Everyone in Matthew's list is a sinner—everyone except one. At the grand climax of this genealogy, there is one who is the Son of God, the holy one, the sinless one. He is placed at the grand climax to give hope to Abraham, David, Judah, Jacob, Tamar, Rahab, Bathsheba, and Ruth. And now for us also there is a Savior. Do you now see the glory and the wonder of this genealogy? Jesus was born of Abraham, David, and Mary to save them and us.

A Break in the "Begats"

There is another abnormality we notice in this genealogy. In the King James Version of this text, we see the word "begat" repeated thirty-nine times: "Abraham begat Isaac; and Isaac begat Jacob," and so on. The New International Version translates it as "Abraham was the father of Isaac, Isaac the father of Jacob," and so on. The Greek word gennaō appears forty times in Matthew 1:1–16. It is used thirty-nine times in the active voice to express the begetting or fathering activity of the male parent, which is the impregnating of the female ovum. Almost every person in this genealogy was born due to the begetting activity of a male human parent. But then we read, "And Jacob the father of Joseph, the husband of Mary, of whom was born Jesus, who is called Christ" (v. 16).

In the King James Version we read, "Jacob begat Joseph." Then what do we expect? "Joseph begat Jesus through Mary," in keeping with the pattern. But here the pattern breaks down. The text simply says, "Jacob begat Joseph, the husband of Mary, of whom was born Jesus, who is called Christ." In this verse Matthew suddenly breaks the "begat" pattern and tells us in no uncertain terms that Joseph did not father, or beget, Jesus. So we see that in his fortieth usage of the word gennaō, Matthew uses it in the passive voice: "of whom was born Jesus, who is called Christ." It is called the divine passive.

28

If you have only the English text, you may question to whom the phrase *"of whom"* refers. It is possible that some might infer from the English text that it could refer to Joseph as well as to Mary. But Greek is more precise, and in the Greek text we see that "of whom" is in the feminine form. That fixes the meaning and leaves no room for doubt. Jesus was born of Mary, not of Joseph. So notice this anomaly, this abnormality, this breaking down of the pattern. Joseph did not beget Jesus. Jesus was born of Mary by a supernatural action.

Who, then, acted to bring about this pregnancy? We find the answer beginning in Matthew 1:18: "His mother Mary was pledged to be married to Joseph, but before they came together, she was found to be with child through the Holy Spirit." And in Matthew 1:20 we read, "An angel of the Lord appeared to him in a dream and said, 'Joseph son of David, do not be afraid to take Mary home as your wife, because what is conceived in her is from the Holy Spirit.'"

In Matthew 1:23, Matthew quotes Isaiah's prophecy: "The virgin will be with child and will give birth to a son, and they will call him Immanuel" (Isa. 7:14). Again, the emphasis is not on Joseph as the father of Jesus. Finally, we read in Matthew 1:25: "But he had no union with her until she gave birth to a son." In all these ways, Matthew is saying that the begetting of Jesus Christ was supernatural and resulted in a virgin birth.

The Virgin Birth of Christ

God interrupts the pattern of "begats" to emphasize the supernatural character of the virgin birth. Unlike everyone else, Jesus Christ was born because of the supernatural activity of the Holy Spirit in the person of Mary. He was conceived by the power of the Holy Ghost. In fact, in Luke 1:35 we are told he is the holy one—the one without sin. Paul says Jesus "had no sin" (2 Cor. 5:21) and that God sent his Son "in the likeness of sinful man" (Rom. 8:3). Paul is telling us that Jesus was without sin and yet he had a body.

Why did Jesus have to be without sin? The Hebrews writer tells us, "Such a high priest meets our need—one who is holy, blameless, pure, set apart from sinners, exalted above the heavens.

Unlike the other high priests, he does not need to offer sacrifices day after day, first for his own sins" (Heb. 7:26–27). He had no sins. He was holy, blameless, and set apart from sinners.

We must have a God/man who is without sin at the climax of this genealogy so that Abraham, David, Judah, Tamar, and all of us can look to him and be saved. Jesus Christ is the eternal Son of God. As we read in John's gospel, "In the beginning was the Word, and the Word was with God, and the Word was God. . . . The Word became flesh and made his dwelling among us. We have seen his glory . . ." (John 1:1, 14). The incarnation of Christ did not in any way diminish his deity, but the divine person did acquire a sinless, permanent human soul and body through Mary. God became flesh for our salvation.

What Do the Divisions Mean?

As we said before, there are three divisions in this genealogy. In verse 17, Matthew emphasizes that he divided the names into fourteen-generation sections. Why is the list organized in this manner?

Some people say it is arranged this way so that people could memorize it. Others say that fourteen is the value of the name of David. In the Hebrew language, letters were also symbols for numbers, and so every word had a numerical value. The Hebrew of Matthew's time did not involve vowels, which are a late invention, so the name of David consisted of three consonants: D, W, and D. The value of D is four, and the value of W is six, so the value of the name David is fourteen. Perhaps, then, Matthew was speaking about the central importance of David, and of the Son of David. Matthew is telling us that Jesus is the great David and David's son.

The first division is from Abraham to David the king. This section speaks about the rise of the glory of Israel under the kingship of David. He was the warrior king who conquered all his enemies and established Israel. The second division is from David to the exile in Babylon. This section speaks of the decline of the glory of Israel. The third section is from the exile to Jesus. This section speaks of the eclipse of the glory of the kingdom of Israel. It reflects the passage of six centuries since the loss of the throne.

As Matthew wrote his gospel, Israel was still, in effect, in exile. Some Jews had returned to their land, yet they were still living under the domination of Rome. So there was a question: Where was the throne of David that was to endure forever in his offspring, as God had promised long ago? Had God abandoned his covenant commitment to Abraham, Jacob, and David? Had God's promise become untrustworthy?

At the climax of the genealogy, there is the phrase "*Jesus, who is called Christ*" (v. 16). What does that say to us, and what did it say to the people of Matthew's time? It indicates the rising glory of Israel after the eclipse of six hundred years. It assures us that God is faithful and his promise sure. In Jesus Christ, the Son of David, the great warrior king has come, and he will defeat all his enemies. The utter defeat of sin, Satan, and death is revealed in these final words of the genealogy, "*and Jacob, the father of Joseph, the husband of Mary, of whom was born Jesus, who is called Christ*" (v. 16). *Christ* is the Greek equivalent of the Hebrew word *Messiah*, meaning one who is anointed and set apart for a God-ordained role.

Do you remember what Gabriel said to Mary? "The Lord God will give him the throne of his father David, and he will reign over the house of Jacob forever; his kingdom will never end" (Luke 1:32–33). After six hundred years, the sun rose with healing in its wings in the person of Jesus, the son of Mary, the son of David, the son of Abraham.

The Seed of the Woman

What else do we learn from this genealogy? Jesus is the seed of the woman (Gal. 3:16–19). Long ago, the Lord God promised Satan, "I will put enmity between you and the woman, and between your offspring [seed] and hers; he will crush your head, and you will strike his heel" (Gen. 3:15). This seed of the woman we recognize as the seed of Abraham, the seed of Judah, the seed of David, and the holy seed of the woman Mary. This seed of the woman who crushes the head of Satan is now identified as Jesus. On the cross, he said, "It is finished," and Paul says Jesus defeated all authorities on the cross (Col. 2:15). Jesus destroyed death in behalf of us by his death and brought us life eternal. In

John 16:33, he told his disciples to cheer up and rejoice because he had overcome the world—he who is the son of Abraham, the son of David, Jesus, who is called Christ.

The True King

Why did Matthew place this genealogical list in the opening chapter of his gospel? He did so to prove beyond the shadow of doubt that Jesus is the son of David, whose kingdom shall be forever. The Jews implied that Jesus was somehow illegitimate (John 8:41), but here Matthew gives us a clear genealogical record that speaks about the pedigree of Christ.

In New Testament times, genealogical records were probably kept by the Sanhedrin, and it is said that these records were available throughout the first century. It is interesting that no one dared to challenge the claim of Jesus that he was the Messiah. They could have easily done so by going to the public record repository and finding evidence that Jesus was not the legal heir to the throne. But no one challenged him on that point because the record was clear: Joseph was of the house of David (Luke 2:4), a son of David through Solomon. Joseph adopted Jesus, who was born of Mary. Therefore Jesus was a legal heir to David's throne because Joseph, a son of David, was Jesus' legal father by adoption. There was no doubt that Jesus was the son of David.

But Matthew was also proclaiming that Jesus was the Christ, the promised Messiah. Peter said that God made Jesus both Lord and Christ (Acts 2:36). Paul said that Jesus was, "as to his human nature . . . a descendant of David" (Rom. 1:3). Paul also said, "Remember Jesus Christ, raised from the dead, descended from David," meaning he was king (2 Tim. 2:8). Jesus himself declared, "I am the Root and the Offspring of David, and the bright Morning Star" (Rev. 22:16). He was speaking about the Isaianic prophecy of the Messiah, a shoot coming out of the stump of Jesse.

Jesus Christ: The Meaning of History

Do you recognize the glory of this genealogy? At the end of it is Jesus Christ. Jesus is the meaning of history; without him, there is no meaning. But notice, this genealogy does not say one word about the Pharaohs of Egypt or the kings of Nineveh, Babylon, or Medo-Persia. It does not say one thing about Alexander the Great or Caesar Augustus. The meaning of history is found in Jesus Christ alone. He is the son of David, the seed of David, the great warrior and conqueror, who goes out conquering and to conquer all his enemies and who rules with an iron scepter. He is the Savior of the world and the King of all nations.

What meaning does Jesus have for us? He will save us. Over and over again we read in the gospels how people cried out to him and were saved. Remember the Canaanite woman whose daughter was demonized? She was a Gentile, but when she came to Jesus she cried, "Lord, Son of David, have mercy upon me!" Both she and her daughter received mercy (Matt. 15:21–28). When the two blind men saw Jesus coming, they cried out, "Lord, Son of David, have mercy on us!" and they received mercy instantly (Matt. 20:29–34).

Do you believe in this genealogy? Do you believe in the identity of Jesus Christ as recorded by Matthew? Let me assure you, it matters if you believe or not. Why? Because there is no other name under heaven given among men by which we may be saved. Jesus said, "I am the way and the truth and the life. No one comes to the Father except through me" (John 14:6). One day, as Jacob prophesied, the obedience of the nations will be Christ's. Jacob was not just speaking about one nation, but all the nations. As the Samaritan people said, "He is the Savior of the world" (John 4:42).

What wonder, what grandeur, what majesty, what greatness abides in this name that is given to us at the end of the list! And he saved some who were in the list, including his own mother. May we think about the claim made here. May we join the Canaanite woman and the blind men and cry out to him: "Lord, Son of David, Jesus, have mercy upon me!" By the mercies of God, I beseech you to put your trust in this Savior who alone is able to save to the uttermost.

4
Do You Want to Be Rich?

MATTHEW 1:18–25

20"Joseph son of David, do not be afraid to take Mary home as your wife, because what is conceived in her is from the Holy Spirit. 21 She will give birth to a son, and you are to give him the name Jesus, because he will save his people from their sins."

Matthew 1:20–21

What is Christmas? Christmas points to Jesus Christ—his person and work of salvation. When we understand what Christmas is, and when we put our faith in Jesus, we will be saved and made rich in spiritual things.

Our heavenly Father sent his eternal Son, our Lord Jesus Christ, into this sinful world, wrapped in sinless human flesh, to save his elect poor sinners by his atoning death on the cross. It is only by faith in Jesus, the only Savior of the whole world, that we may be justified and adopted as children of God to enjoy fellowship with God in eternal happiness.

This Jesus, the very rich Son of God, became very poor in his incarnation so that we may become spiritually very rich in him. That is what I am, and that is what you are—very rich in things that matter, if we have trusted in Christ.

Saints, we are rich, not in silver or gold, but in salvation and in eternal life, which only Jesus can give. The angel told Joseph, *"You are to give him the name Jesus, because he will save his people from their sins"* (v. 21). Jesus is our heavenly Father's indescribable gift to us.

Have you unpacked this gift? Have you put your trust in Christ? Have you received Jesus as your Savior and Lord? Are you rich in him? God is not interested in our money or degrees. The only thing that matters is whether we have trusted in Christ alone. Paul writes, "For you know the grace of our Lord Jesus Christ, that though he was rich, yet for your sakes he became poor, so that you through his poverty might become rich" (2 Cor. 8:9). He also exclaims, "Thanks be to God for his indescribable gift!" (2 Cor. 9:15).

If we have trusted in Christ, we are truly rich. In Revelation 2, we read, "To the angel of the church in Smyrna write: These are the words of him who is the First and the Last, who died and came to life again. I know your afflictions and your poverty—yet you are rich!" (Rev. 2:8–9). Later, the Lord told the Laodicean church, "You say, 'I am rich; I have acquired wealth and do not need a thing.'" This is what many people in this country also say. But the Lord continued, "But you do not realize that you are wretched, pitiful, poor, blind and naked. I counsel you to buy from me gold refined in the fire, so you can become rich; and white clothes to wear, so you can cover your shameful nakedness; and salve to put on your eyes, so you can see" (Rev. 3:17–18).

Listen to the counsel Christ gave to a rich man in Luke 12. The man said, "I'll say to myself, 'You have plenty of good things laid up for many years. Take life easy; eat, drink and be merry.'" But God told him, "You fool! This very night your life will be demanded from you. Then who will get what you have prepared for yourself?" Jesus concluded, "This is how it will be with anyone who stores up things for himself but is not rich toward God" (Luke 12:19–21).

What, then, is Christmas? We find the answer in the Bible. I do not believe in the so-called "spirit of Christmas," Santa Claus, or "Jingle Bells." But I believe in the birth of Jesus Christ, God's eternal Son, in Bethlehem, as foretold by the Lord through his holy prophets. I believe in Jesus Christ, one divine Person in two natures: holy God and sinless human. He is the only Savior of the world, who made atonement for our sins. Everyone who believes in him shall be saved.

The gift that the heavenly Father has given us is the unspeakable gift of the Savior, Jesus, the eternal Son of God. The question is, have you received him? Have you trusted in him? And, additionally, have you proclaimed him to your children that they may also believe in him?

This Savior, Jesus Christ, was begotten of the Holy Spirit and born of the virgin Mary, as the Lord had promised over seven hundred years earlier through the prophet Isaiah. During this season, the true church celebrates the birth of this virgin-born child, the Mighty God, the Son of David, the everlasting King, the shoot out of the stump of Jesse, as well as the root of Jesse, the liberator of all our burdens, and the Savior of the world.

The Gospel Introductions

How do the gospels introduce this Jesus to us? In their narratives, Matthew and Luke call him the virgin-born Savior, the Lord Christ Jesus, the Holy One, the Son of the Most High, the Son of God, and Immanuel. Mark does not give us an account of his birth as Matthew and Luke do, but he does introduce him as Jesus, the Son of God.

1. John's Account

What about John? In his prologue in the first chapter, John introduces Jesus to us by saying, first, "In the beginning was the Word" (John 1:1). In his book *Knowing God*, J. I. Packer tells us that this verse speaks of the eternity of the Lord Jesus Christ.[2] When other things began, he already existed. In other words, Jesus Christ is eternal.

John continues, "and the Word was with God." This speaks about Christ's personality. This Word is a personal being, an eternal personality, distinct from the Father and yet eternally in fellowship with God the Father. Then John says, "and the Word was God." That speaks about the deity of the Word. He is God, and yet he is personally distinct from the Father.

Then we read, "Through him all things were made; without him nothing was made that has been made" (John 1:3). John is telling us that the Word is also the Creator of all things, visible and invisible. He created all, yet he himself was not part of

2 J. I. Packer, *Knowing God* (Downers Grove, IL: InterVarsity, 1993), 66.

creation. Then we are told, "In him was life" (John 1:4). By this John tells us the origin of all life must be seen in Jesus Christ. Additionally, it tells us the cause of the continuation of all life must also be seen in this Word who is God, Jesus Christ.

So John says, "In him was life, and that life was the light of men" (John 1:4). Not only is Jesus the author and sustainer of all life, but the true knowledge of God also comes to us only through Jesus Christ. There is no other way we can know God except through Jesus.

Then John says, "The Word became flesh and made his dwelling among us" (John 1:14). John understands that Jesus Christ is the eternal Word, the personal Being distinct from the Father, God himself, the Creator and Author of all life and the Author of all revelation of God. This God, this Creator, this Word-become-flesh, the mighty God, once lay helplessly as a baby in a cattle-feeding trough. But John has no doubt who this One is: "We have seen his glory, the glory of the One and Only [the only Begotten], who came from the Father, full of grace and truth" (John 1:14). Finally, John writes, "No one has ever seen God, but God the One and Only, who is at the Father's side, has made him known" (John 1:18). Thus John introduces Jesus Christ to us: God became flesh.

2. MATTHEW'S ACCOUNT

The accounts of the birth of Christ as found in the gospels of Matthew and Luke are quite detailed. When we examine them, we notice that they are independent of each other. Yet they concur in this great doctrine of the virgin birth.

First, in Matthew's account, Matthew tells us that Joseph had nothing to do with the begetting of Jesus. Matthew's genealogical list ends with "Jacob the father of Joseph, the husband of Mary, of whom was born Jesus, who is called Christ" (Matt. 1:16). Then Matthew gives a further explanation: *"This is how the birth of Jesus Christ came about: His mother Mary was pledged to be married to Joseph, but before they came together, she was found to be with child through the Holy Spirit [ek pneumatos hagiou]"* (Matt. 1:18).

Then we read that an angel was commissioned to come to Joseph at night in a dream. To correct Joseph's wrong assumption, the angel told him about the supernatural aspect of this pregnancy:

"Joseph son of David, do not be afraid to take Mary home as your wife, because what is conceived in her is from the Holy Spirit [ek pneumatos hagiou]" (Matt. 1:20). The Holy Spirit begat, and Mary conceived and gave birth.

Matthew continues, "All this took place so that the word of the Lord might be fulfilled." What was that word? *"The virgin will be with child and will give birth to a son, and they will call him Immanuel'—which means, 'God with us'"* (Matt. 1:22–23). I agree with James Orr and J. Gresham Machen and a number of others that the prophecy of Isaiah 7:14 has a singular reference. This prophecy is speaking about the birth of Christ through the virgin Mary by the power of the Holy Spirit.

Thus, Matthew, under the inspiration of the Holy Spirit, who also inspired Isaiah to write his prophecy, says that the events of Christ's birth took place in fulfillment of what the Lord had spoken through Isaiah. Jesus was born of a virgin. And in verse 25, Matthew goes out of his way to let us know that Joseph did not have any sexual relationship with Mary until this son was born. This refutes the idea of Mary's perpetual virginity (see also Matt. 13:55–56).

Finally, Matthew says, *"[Joseph] gave him the name Jesus"* (Matt. 1:25). Giving Jesus his name meant that Joseph was adopting Jesus as his son and becoming his legal father. Joseph is addressed here as the son of David, which means that he was a prince, although the Davidic dynasty had declined and was in eclipse. So we see that out of the stump of Jesse's line came a shoot, a branch, who is Jesus. He became the legal heir to David's throne through Joseph, a son of David, and through Joseph's adopting him. Note that both Joseph and Mary were descended from David.

3. LUKE'S ACCOUNT

Luke also gives us clear evidence of the virgin birth of Christ. In Luke 1:27, Mary is called a virgin, *hē parthenos*. In fact, Luke uses the word "virgin" twice in that verse. And in Luke 1:34, this young girl, the virgin Mary, asks, "How can this be since I do not know a man?" She meant "to know a man sexually." The angel's answer was that the Holy Spirit would come upon her: "The power of the Most High will overshadow you." Then Gabriel added that there is nothing impossible with God (Luke 1:35, 37).

Was Luke making all this up? No. Luke was a historian who was interested only in the truth. In the beginning of his gospel he wrote, "Many have undertaken to draw up an account of the things that have been fulfilled among us" (Luke 1:1). Luke was not setting out to write mythology, or fake news. He was a historian whose purpose was to write the things that took place, "just as they were handed down to us by those who from the first were eyewitnesses" (Luke 1:2). There is no question that the source for both Matthew and Luke for this account of the virgin birth was Mary herself. Luke said that he interviewed "eyewitnesses and servants of the word," those who had seen the events he was recording.

Luke also stated, "I myself have carefully investigated everything from the beginning" (Luke 1:3). His intent was not to write a novel, creating a story from his head. He was a historian who personally investigated all things about Christ "from the beginning," which included the virgin birth. And because of his investigations, he told his readers, "It seemed good also to me to write an orderly account . . . so that you may know the certainty of the things you have been taught" (Luke 1:3–4). Luke wanted his readers to know that Christianity rests upon indisputable historical facts.

So Luke began his gospel account, first, by the narration of the supernatural birth of John the Baptist, and, second, with the supernatural virgin birth of Jesus Christ. Therefore, we must understand that the virgin birth is historical and factual. It is recorded so that we may have certainty of the gospel. Without the virgin birth, there is no gospel.

An Essential Doctrine

Some people, such as the late Professor William Barclay, a Scottish scholar, and many others, consider the birth of Jesus Christ as "a crude fact."[3] They do not see any beauty in the virgin birth. In his study on Matthew, Barclay tells us that the virgin birth is a doctrine that presents us with many difficulties. Then he says, "And our Church [he was speaking about his own church] does not compel us to accept it in the literal and physical sense."[4]

---

3   William Barclay, *The Gospel of Matthew*, Vol. 1, Daily Study Bible Series, rev. ed., (Philadelphia: Westminster, 1975), 23.

4   Barclay, *The Gospel of Matthew*, 20.

Isn't that wonderful? We have come a long way. The creeds all state that the virgin birth of Christ is an essential part of the Christian faith. But Barclay says his church would not compel him, or anyone else, to believe in the virgin birth of Christ in a literal, physical sense, although, as a scholar, Barclay knew that the Bible teaches a literal, physical virgin birth. Thus, Barclay states, "This is one of the doctrines on which the Church says that we have full liberty to come to our own conclusion."[5] Barclay and those who agree with him are saying that we do not have to believe what the Bible clearly teaches, because we are living in the modern scientific age. They are saying Christians should no longer believe in the "primitive" concept of miracles.

But to me, and to this church, and to millions of orthodox, Bible-believing Christians around the world, the virgin birth of Jesus is not a crude, ugly fact. To us who believe in God as the Creator of the heavens and the earth, believing in miracles is not a problem at all. It is a mark of true intelligence, of divine wisdom. Paul says, "We have the mind of Christ" (1 Cor. 2:16). So we glory in the virgin birth of Jesus, the second Person of the Godhead, because without the virgin birth, the cross would be emptied of its power. Without the virgin birth, Jesus would be just a sinful man, not able to save anyone. He himself would need a savior. If we remove the virgin birth, then we remove the power of the cross to save us, even though, in the cross of Christ, the infinite wisdom of God is made manifest (see 1 Cor. 1:18–25).

The church of Jesus Christ has always believed in the virgin birth, as we read in her creeds. This doctrine is essential to our salvation. So, unlike William Barclay and his church, our church believes, teaches, and glories in the biblical doctrine of the virgin birth of Jesus. If we deny the virgin birth, we will soon begin to deny all the miracles of the Bible. We will reduce Jesus to a mere man, albeit a nice, ethical one. In fact, we may even say he is the best man who ever lived, but still a man, incapable of saving anyone. What does such reductionism do? It removes the meaning of Christmas by removing the Savior.

Let us consider what pious scholars like J. Gresham Machen, the New Testament scholar and founder of Westminster Theological

---

5   Ibid.

Seminary, said: "Our salvation depends squarely upon history; the Bible contains that history, and unless that history is true the authority of the Bible is gone and we who have put our trust in the Bible are without hope. . . . Those who reject the virgin birth reject the whole supernatural view of Christ." And I say, "Those who reject the supernatural cannot be true Christians, and cannot have the life of God in the soul of man." Machen also explains that a man is saved by grace through faith in Jesus Christ "as he is offered to us in the gospel."[6] Part of that gospel is the stupendous miracle of the virgin birth. Professor B. B. Warfield of Princeton said, "The supernatural Christ and the supernatural salvation carry with them by an inevitable consequence, the supernatural birth"[7] of Christ.

What does God say about his word? Jesus said, "Sanctify them by the truth; your word is truth" (John 17:17). Paul wrote, "Let God be true and all men liars" (Rom. 3:4). The psalmist says, "The words of the LORD are flawless, like silver refined in a furnace of clay, purified seven times" (Ps. 12:6). He also says, "The law of the LORD is perfect, reviving the soul. The statutes of the LORD are trustworthy, making wise the simple" (Ps. 19:7).

The so-called "wise" people of the world believe that the Bible is not true and that we must demythologize it, as Rudolf Bultmann did, by rejecting all miracles. They say that we must not permit God to act in his world and they believe the lie of a closed system of a chance universe. But these are all lies.

Joseph Makes a Decision

Luke's detailed account of the birth of Jesus Christ gives clear evidence of his belief in the virgin birth. After Mary received the angelic announcement in Nazareth, she was overshadowed by the Holy Spirit and she conceived. Mary then went from Nazareth to Judea to visit Elizabeth to receive spiritual encouragement and enjoy fellowship with her. After three months, Mary returned to Nazareth, and Joseph learned of Mary's pregnancy. Probably she

6   J. Gresham Machen, *The Virgin Birth of Christ* (Grand Rapids: Baker, 1965), 385, 391, 396.

7   B. B. Warfield, *Christology and Criticism*, Vol. 3 of *Works of B. B. Warfield* (Grand Rapids: Baker, 1981), 452.

said to him, "I am with child by the power of the Holy Spirit, according to the word of a holy angel, Gabriel." But Joseph did not believe Mary's explanation.

In Jewish society of that time, marriage consisted of, first, a betrothal in which the couple exchanged vows of fidelity before witnesses. From that point on, the man was known as husband and the woman as wife. This was the first phase of marriage. But before the couple lived together as husband and wife, there was a period of about one year. At the end of the year, the husband would come to his bride's father's house and ceremoniously take his bride to his own home in a celebration such as we read about in Matthew 25. After the marriage feast, the couple would live together as husband and wife.

Mary informed Joseph that she was pregnant. Being a just man, Joseph refused to marry her. At the same time, he desired to divorce her privately by writing her a bill of divorce before two witnesses and letting her go, as permitted in Deuteronomy 24:1.

What was Mary doing during this time? She was trusting in the Lord to solve this great, thorny problem with Joseph. In my view, she probably reasoned, "Nothing is impossible with God. As Gabriel stated, I am pregnant with the Holy Child by the supernatural work of the Holy Spirit." So she concluded, "This problem is God's problem. He must solve it, and he will solve it. I must trust God" (see Luke 1:38).

God's Solution

In time, God sent an angel to Joseph also. I am sure Joseph loved Mary. Yet he did not think that he could go through with the marriage. After deciding to divorce Mary privately, Joseph went to bed. I am sure that before he went to bed, he prayed. He probably said, "O God, take care of this matter. I only want to do what is right in accordance with your law."

The angel of the Lord came and spoke to Joseph in a dream that night. He brought a command from the Lord. The angel told Joseph, *"Do not be afraid to take Mary home as your wife"* (Matt. 1:20). God wanted Joseph to go ahead with the second part of his marriage and to bring Mary ceremoniously to his house, to have the marriage feast, and then begin to take care of her. Then

God revealed the truth to Joseph about Mary: *"What is conceived in her is from the Holy Spirit"* (v. 20).

When Joseph heard these words, the darkness was dispelled from his mind. The angel was saying that Mary was not an adulteress. She was a virgin—innocent, just, righteous, and pure. In other words, this pregnancy was God's work. Joseph did love Mary, so you can imagine the great joy that filled his soul as he heard these words. Mary had trusted God, and he solved her problem. Nothing is impossible with God.

Then the angel gave further instructions, *"She will give birth to a son, and you are to give him the name Jesus"* (v. 21). In other words, Joseph must protect Mary, honor her, and provide for her. He must adopt this son by naming him, which was an official act. Thus, Joseph would become the legal father of Jesus. As we said, Joseph was the prince, the son of David, a legal heir to the throne. Now, by being named and adopted by Joseph, Jesus would also become a legal heir to the throne of David. He is King Jesus, whose kingdom is everlasting.

Notice how Joseph went to bed with one decision and woke up with God's decision. How many times do we decide without facts or understanding? I tell people, "Go and pray," and often they come back and say, "I prayed." But I do not know what they really did. Prayer means going to God and saying, "God, show me your way, your decision. I have already decided, but my decision does not have to be right. What is your decision?" It may surprise us to discover that sometimes God's decision is the opposite of the decision we have made.

Joseph accepted God's guidance and changed his previous decision to divorce Mary. He took her for his wife and began to protect her, provide for her, and honor her. And when she gave birth, he dutifully adopted her son and gave him the name Jesus. Notice the obedience of Joseph. He obeyed immediately, exactly, and joyfully.

The Purpose of the Virgin Birth

Who is Jesus? The angel told Joseph to name him Jesus, *"because he will save his people from their sins"* (v. 21). I offer this Jesus to you: he is the only one who can save us from our sins. Soon we must die and face judgment. The Bible says, "Now is the time of God's favor, now is the day of salvation" (2 Cor. 6:2).

The Greek text tells us that Jesus alone will save his people from their sins. There is no other savior. We have the freedom in this country to believe whatever we want. But there is no other savior outside of Christ. Jesus alone will save his people. He said, "I am the way and the truth and the life. No one comes to the Father except through me" (John 14:6). He is the only mediator between God and man.

Here, then, is revealed the purpose of this virgin birth: God is giving us a Savior who is able to save his people from their sins by his atoning death. Jesus came to save his elect people, whom the Father had given him in eternity that he may save them.[8]

The psalmist tells us, "No man can redeem the life of another or give to God a ransom for him—the ransom for a life is costly, no payment is ever enough" (Ps. 49:7–8). All the wealth in the world cannot save one soul. Then the psalmist says, "But God will redeem my life from the grave; he will surely take me to himself" (Ps. 49:15). And in Psalm 130:7–8 we find another reference to what is stated in Matthew 1: "O Israel, put your hope in the LORD, for with the LORD is unfailing love and with him is full redemption. He himself will redeem Israel from all their sins." That is what we read in Matthew 1: *"Give him the name Jesus, for he [and he alone] will save his people from their sins"* (v. 21). How do you know who "his people" are? If you repent and trust in him, you are his people, eternally chosen in Christ to belong to him. And if you refuse to repent and believe, your refusal demonstrates that you are not his people.

In the fullness of time, God, through the virgin birth, gave us a sinless Savior who is God/man, able to redeem us from our sins. Joseph was told to name him Jesus, for he alone would save his people, whether Jews or Gentiles, rich or poor, male or female, from their sins. "Jesus" was a common name during New Testament times; anyone could name his child Jesus. It is taken from the Hebrew verb *yasha*, which means "to save and deliver" from danger, sickness, and death. But the problem is, can any person save another from these problems? And who can deliver us from the greatest problem of all, which is our sin?

---

8   See the Westminster Confession of Faith, chapter 8, sections 1 and 2.

Man's Fundamental Problem

Peter said there is only one Savior, the Lord Jesus Christ. He said, "Salvation is found in no one else, for there is no other name under heaven given to men by which we must be saved" (Acts 4:12). What does Jesus save his people from? He saves us from our sins. Let me assure you, the fundamental problem of man is not political, economic, social, medical, or educational. Man's fundamental problem is his sin. He is by nature an enemy of God. Sin is the cause of all human sufferings and all other problems (see Rom. 5:12).

In Genesis 3, we see how sin came into humanity. Adam sinned, and, through him, we all are sinners. We are conceived in sin, born in sin, and practice sin daily. We must never say that we are not sinners, or that we do not need Jesus to save us. If we do, he will deal with us severely. He is the one who saves but he is also the one who judges. All people will go either to heaven or to hell.

Our hearts are the problem. The prophet Jeremiah declares that our hearts are deceitful above all things and desperately wicked (Jer. 17:9). Paul says that no one seeks God, all have gone astray, and there is no fear of God in man (Rom. 3:9–18).

Jesus also spoke about the wickedness of the human heart: "For out of the heart come evil thoughts, murder, adultery, sexual immorality, theft, false testimony, slander" (Matt. 15:19). In the depths of their hearts, all people are enemies of God and cut off from the life of God. Sin separates man from God. But Jesus came to solve our sin problem and reconcile us to God through his death on the cross.

Jesus alone is perfect God and perfect, sinless man; therefore, only Jesus could give his life as a ransom for many (Matt. 20:28). Only the Christ of Christianity can save sinners. In Matthew 26:28, while instituting the holy supper, Jesus said, "This is my blood of the covenant, which is poured out for many for the forgiveness of sins." There is no other way to save people from their sins except by the sinless God/man coming into the world and dying on the cross.

Paul says, "God made him who had no sin to be sin for us, so that in him we might become the righteousness of God"

(2 Cor. 5:21). Elsewhere he writes, "Christ died for our sins" (1 Cor. 15:3).

The one who lay helplessly in the cattle trough in Bethlehem is the almighty God-become-flesh. He died on the cross for sinners that he may redeem his people, Jews and Gentiles, from their sins. God's covenant with Abraham was that in his offspring all the families of the earth would be blessed. Paul says Christ loved the church and gave himself for her (Eph. 5:25). Therefore, the elect people of God by grace will surely repent, believe on the Lord Jesus Christ, and be saved. Jesus will save *all* his people.

The Fullness of Salvation

What does salvation mean? First, it means salvation from sin— from the guilt of sin, the pollution of sin, the power of sin, the punishment of sin, and even the presence of sin. Our problem is sin, and it is dealt with totally and comprehensively by Jesus Christ.

Second, it means that we are saved to serve God, to enjoy life eternal. The purpose of salvation is that we may have fellowship with God and his Son Jesus Christ our Lord, as we read in John 17:3, "Now this is eternal life: that they may know you, the only true God, and Jesus Christ, whom you have sent." The virgin-born Christ obeyed God fully. He died on the cross in behalf of our sins and gave us eternal life. This is God's only way of saving sinners.

God looked at man and saw his problem. So he sent a Savior, his only Son, to solve our sin problem and to bring us back into joyful fellowship with him. God says to all of us, "I know your problem. It is your heart. You are a rebel who is cut off from God. The solution to your problem is through my Son, the Savior, King Jesus. Through his death, he will solve your sin problem and reconcile you to me." That is what Jesus did. The good shepherd laid down his life for the sheep. So Paul explains, "Therefore, there is now no condemnation for those who are in Christ Jesus" (Rom. 8:1).

Any attempt at self-redemption by a sinner is utterly foolish and impossible. God gave us a Savior from heaven. Paul says Jesus is "the second man, the man from heaven" (see 1 Cor. 15:45–49), and Matthew tells us he is Immanuel, "God with us." Jesus is God, and Jesus is with us always. So fear not, friends. He who is with us and in us is greater than the devil, who is in the world. In Jesus Christ, we are more than conquerors.

Receiving God's Gift

In conclusion, I must ask you two extremely serious questions. First, have you received this personal gift from the Father? Second, have you given this gift to your children? We must think about these things. Why? This one is Immanuel, God with us. Jesus said, "Surely I am with you always, to the very end of the age" (Matt. 28:20). He is our good shepherd, and so we lack nothing. He is with us in life, in death, and beyond.

Truly, to us a child is born, a son is given, for our salvation, and for our joy. The Word became flesh and dwelt among us. Professor William Hendriksen says that Christ came to dwell "with the sick to heal them." He came to dwell "with the demon-possessed, to liberate them." He came to dwell "with the poor in spirit . . . to bless them," and I would add, to make them very rich. He came to dwell "with the care-ridden, to rid them of care." He came to dwell "with lepers, to cleanse them." He came to dwell "with the diseased, to cure them." He came to dwell "with the hungry, to feed them," not only with physical bread but with the living bread. And above all, he came to dwell "with the lost, to seek and save them."[9]

Jesus is *nobiscum Deus*, the "with-us God." He has already come to be with us in the person of Jesus Christ. And yet a greater reality awaits us at his second coming. John tells us of this *nobiscum Deus* coming in his fullness:

> Then I saw a new heaven and a new earth, for the first heaven and the first earth had passed away, and there was no longer any sea. I saw the Holy City, the new Jerusalem, coming down out of heaven from God, prepared as a bride beautifully dressed for her husband. And I heard a loud voice from the throne saying, "Now the dwelling of God is with men, and he will live with them. They will be his people, and God himself will be with

---

9   William Hendriksen, *Exposition of the Gospel according to Matthew*, New Testament Commentary series (Grand Rapids: Baker, 1989), 141.

them and be their God. He will wipe every tear from their eyes. There will be no more death or mourning or crying or pain, for the old order of things has passed away." (Rev. 21:1–4)

The late Professor Eta Linnemann of Germany gave several theological lectures in this church in 2001. She had attended the universities of Marburg, Tübingen, and Göttingen. She studied under Professor Rudolf Bultmann, the father of demythologization, as well as under Ernst Fuchs, Friedrich Gogarten, Gerhard Ebeling, and others. She wrote books in defense of the unbelieving historical-criticism. Then Jesus saved her. So she counseled people to burn all her books that had been written in defense of rationalism. Consider her words: "My 'No!' to historical-critical theology stems from my 'Yes!' to my wonderful Lord and Savior, Jesus Christ, and to the glorious redemption he accomplished for me on Golgotha."[10]

Friends, I am speaking to you eternal matters. Can you rejoice because God in Jesus Christ is with us? Or do you still refuse to believe that he is the eternal God who became perfect man, the divine Person who took to himself a perfect human nature so that in it he may die on the cross for our salvation? Ask yourself: Why did he clothe himself with human flesh? He became man so that he could die on the cross for our sins. The wages of sin is death. Christ died for my sins, and my sins are totally forgiven. I am justified and adopted into the family of God.

If you are not trusting in Christ, may God have mercy on you! May he help you to hope in nothing else and in no one else but in God's Son alone. He alone is our Savior and our Lord. He alone is the Son of the Most High, the Holy One. He alone can make us rich with eternal salvation. So if you have trusted in Christ, you can rejoice greatly. But if you are outside of Christ, may you this day trust in him, this Christmas gift God himself has given. And if you do so, then you can rejoice for the first time in your life and for the rest of your life.

---

10 Eta Linnemann, *Historical Criticism of the Bible: Methodology or Ideology: Reflections of a Bultmannian Turned Evangelical*, trans. by Robert Yarbrough (Grand Rapids: Kregel, 2001), 17.

5
Jesus Christ: God, King, and Savior

MATTHEW 1:18–25

²²All this took place to fulfill what the Lord had said through the prophet: ²³"The virgin will be with child and will give birth to a son, and they will call him Immanuel"—which means, "God with us."

Matthew 1:22–23

Who is Jesus of Nazareth? To many people, Jesus was like any other man. They say he was the son of a biological father, Joseph. They believe he was a religious guru or a revolutionary, but still a man, who lived and died two thousand years ago. But it is about this Jesus that the angel of God made a startling declaration to the poor shepherds of Bethlehem. His words tell us that Jesus of Nazareth was much more than just a man. The angel said, "Do not be afraid. I bring you good news of great joy that will be for all the people. Today in the town of David a Savior has been born to you; he is Christ the Lord" (Luke 2:10–11). He was telling them about the birth of Jesus Christ to the virgin Mary in Bethlehem.

To unbelieving theologians, the virgin birth is the product of the fertile imagination of the evangelists. But the truth is that it is the greatest event that has taken place in history. In fulfillment of the word spoken by the Lord through the prophet Isaiah more than seven hundred years earlier, Jesus Christ was born of Mary in Bethlehem. Through the virgin birth, God became man and dwelt among us.

Jesus Is God

Who is this thumb-sucking baby clothed in swaddling clothes and placed in a manger in Bethlehem? First, he is the true and living God. Other religions may honor Jesus Christ by saying that he was a great prophet, like other human prophets. But this is not true. Other prophets were mere sinful men, while Jesus is a divine sinless person. As John Murray said, "He who never began to be in his specific identity as Son of God, *began* to be what he eternally was not. . . . [In Jesus there was] the conjunction in one person of all that belongs to Godhead and all that belongs to manhood."[11] In him, there are two natures "joined together in one person, without conversion, composition, or confusion."[12]

Jesus Christ is God/man. Professor Murray also said, "The infinite became the finite, the eternal and supratemporal entered time and became subject to its conditions, the immutable became the mutable, the invisible became the visible, the Creator became the created, the sustainer of all became dependent, the Almighty infirm. All is summed up in the proposition, God became man."[13]

Jesus is God and Lord over all the people in the world, no matter what religion they claim. He became man to die so that by his death he might destroy the works of the devil and take away all our sins. But Jesus alone will also be the Judge of all people at the end of time.

In the humanity of Jesus Christ, the Almighty became dependent just as any newborn baby is dependent on others. But we must not be mistaken about this infant who lay in a manger in Bethlehem long ago. Though he was dependent, he is also the Creator and Sustainer of all, the one who sustains all things by his powerful word (Heb. 1:3). Jesus was sustaining the universe even as he was lying as a baby in that manger in Bethlehem. Paul says in reference to him, "By him all things were created: things in heaven and on earth, visible and invisible, whether thrones or powers or rulers or authorities; all things were created by him and for him. He is before all things, and in him all things hold together" (Col. 1:16–17). All

---

11 John Murray, *Collected Writings*, vol. 2, *Systematic Theology* (Edinburgh: Banner of Truth, 1977), 132–133.

12 Westminster Confession of Faith, "Of Christ the Mediator," Ch. 8, section 2.

13 Murray, 132.

things were created by Christ and for him, and in him all things cohere; without Christ all things disintegrate. We are here today as human beings because of his holding us together.

In this baby, "all the fullness of the Deity lives in bodily form" (Col. 2:9). He is Immanuel—the "with-us God" (Matt. 1:23). The phrase "with-us" stands for Christ's human nature. This virgin-conceived baby is none other than God who came to live among us in a human body.

Old Testament References to the Deity of Christ

The entire Old Testament speaks about Christ. For example, long before Jesus was born, Isaiah spoke about his virgin birth: "The virgin will be with child and will give birth to a son, and will call him Immanuel" (Isa. 7:14). Then, in reference to Christ, Isaiah declared, "For to us a child is born, to us a son is given, and the government will be on his shoulders. And he will be called Wonderful Counselor, Mighty God, Everlasting Father, Prince of Peace. Of the increase of his government and peace there will be no end" (Isa. 9:6–7). We find reference to Christ also in Isaiah 11: "A shoot will come up from the stump of Jesse; from his roots a Branch will bear fruit. The Spirit of the LORD will rest on him— the Spirit of wisdom and of understanding, the Spirit of counsel and of power, the Spirit of knowledge and of the fear of the LORD—and he will delight in the fear of the LORD" (Isa. 11:1–3).

The psalmist referred to the work of Christ as Savior as he prayed, "O Israel, put your hope in the LORD, for with the LORD is unfailing love and with him is full redemption. He himself will redeem Israel from all their sins" (Ps. 130:7–8). In Isaiah 43:11, God tells us, "I, even I, am the LORD, and apart from me there is no savior." Thus, we understand from the Old Testament that God will redeem us from all our sins and that God alone is the Savior; apart from him there is no salvation.

New Testament References to the Deity of Christ

The New Testament tells us that this salvation activity will be attributed to one person, Jesus of Nazareth, the baby born in

Bethlehem to Mary and Joseph. So we read the instructions of the angel to Joseph before Jesus' birth, *"You are to give him the name Jesus, because he will save his people from their sins"* (v. 21). This tells us that Jesus the Savior is the God of the Old Testament. If Jesus were not God, he could save no one; but Jesus Christ is God.

The angel Gabriel told Mary that the child she would bear as a virgin would be called "the Son of the Most High," meaning, again, that he is God, the eternal Son (Luke 1:32). When announcing Jesus' birth to the shepherds, the angel identified this infant as "Christ the Lord," using the word *Kurios* ("Lord"), which is the Greek word used for *Yahweh* in the Septuagint (Luke 2:11). By using *Kurios*, the writers of the gospel were saying this infant was God himself. In the same way, the angel was describing the child to be born in Bethlehem in the highest possible terms, saying he would be Savior, Christ, and Lord.

Elizabeth used the same word (*Kurios*) when she made a profound statement about Mary's child: "But why am I so favored, that the mother of my Lord should come to me?" (Luke 1:43). In doing so, Elizabeth was also acknowledging that Mary was the mother of God.

I hope that you who still treat Jesus Christ as a mere man will understand who this baby is and put your trust in him. This baby whose birth we celebrate at Christmas is God himself. When we read in the gospels that Jesus claimed to have authority on earth to forgive sins, some people raised the question, "Who is Jesus to forgive sins? Only God can do that." But Jesus does have authority to forgive sins. Why? Because he is God (Mark 2:6–10).

Jesus Is King

Not only is Jesus God, but he is also King. This infant without a home was legally the son of Joseph, the son of David, as his genealogy tells us. He was begotten in Mary's womb of the Holy Spirit, not of Joseph. Thus, we understand this truth that the Holy Spirit begat, Mary conceived, and Joseph adopted. But, in obedience to God, Joseph named the child Jesus, thus becoming his legal father. So Joseph and Jesus were not biological father and son, but legal father and son; therefore, the throne of David belonged legally to Jesus.

The angel Gabriel spoke to Mary in Nazareth, "He will be great and will be called the Son of the Most High. The Lord God will give him the throne of his father David, and he will reign over the house of Jacob forever; his kingdom will never end" (Luke 1:32–33). This is the fulfillment of the promise that God made to David in 2 Samuel 7:13, 16, and 29. Jesus Christ is David's last son. There are no more kings coming after him, because this Son will never die. His kingdom is for ever and ever.

The Magi inquired, "Where is the one born king of the Jews?" (Matt. 2:2). In Micah 5:2 we read, "But you, Bethlehem Ephrathah, though you are small among the clans of Judah, out of you will come for me one who will be ruler over Israel, whose origins are from of old, from ancient times." Here Jesus, the one whose origins are from eternity, the baby who was born of a virgin in Bethlehem, is presented as the ruler of Israel. In Isaiah 9:6–7 we read, "The government shall be upon his shoulders" and "of the increase of his government and peace there will be no end." No matter what we think, Jesus Christ is God and King.

In Isaiah 11, the rule of Christ is clearly articulated. I hope that we will tremble when we read this. The Lord Jesus Christ is not just a little king in a little town somewhere; rather, he is the King of kings and Lord of lords. So we read, "But with righteousness he will judge the needy, with justice he will give decisions for the poor of the earth" (Isa. 11:4). This One, who is greater than David and Solomon, will judge the world with justice. Isaiah continues, "He will strike the earth with the rod of his mouth; with the breath of his lips he will slay the wicked." The wicked are those who never repent of their sins and put their entire faith in Christ. At the end of time, this Jesus, who is God and King, will do what is spoken here: He will strike the earth with the rod of his mouth and slay the wicked with the breath of his lips.

We also see the kingship of Jesus Christ in his triumphal entry into Jerusalem, which was a fulfillment of Zechariah's prophecy: "Say to the Daughter of Zion, 'See, your king comes to you, gentle and riding on a donkey, on a colt, the foal of a donkey.'" (Matt. 21:4–5).

When Jesus was brought before the Roman governor, Pilate asked him, "'Are you the king of the Jews?' 'Yes, it is as you say,'

Jesus replied" (Matt. 27:11). Here we see in Jesus' own words his claim to be King.

If you are still not convinced of the kingship of Christ, look at his words in Matthew 28:18: "All authority in heaven and on earth has been given to me." All authority! That includes authority to deal with us. Jesus was referring to Daniel's prophecy, where we read,

> In my vision at night I looked, and there before me was one like a son of man, coming with the clouds of heaven. He approached the Ancient of Days and was led into his presence. He was given authority, glory and sovereign power; all peoples, nations and men of every language worshiped him. His dominion is an everlasting dominion that will not pass away, and his kingdom is one that will never be destroyed. (Dan. 7:13–14)

We are all going to die, whether we like it or not. But Jesus lives, and he alone has all authority to raise us up and judge us. We must be careful about how we treat him, for he has been given authority, glory, and sovereign power over all people and nations.

The kingdom of God came, then, in the person of this infant Jesus. That is why he tells us, "Seek first his kingdom and his righteousness" (Matt. 6:33). It means we must put God first in our lives. It means we must come under the rule of this God-King. It means we must confess with our mouths, "Jesus is Lord," and do what he says.

King Jesus is greater than David or Solomon. They were only human beings who represented the great King. David and Solomon represented God as his deputies, but Jesus is the archetype, the ultimate reality. As God and King, he alone is sovereign; he alone can say, "All authority in heaven and on earth is given to me." He alone is King of kings and Lord of lords.

In Isaiah 52:7, we find a prophecy of this Jesus: "How beautiful on the mountains are the feet of those who bring good news." What is the good news? "Your God reigns!"

Jesus Is Savior

So the little baby whose birth we celebrate at Christmas is our God and King. He has come and is reigning, and when he reigns, everything is all right. Additionally, because he is God and King, he is able to save his people.

This God-King Jesus Christ is the Savior of the world. He is the one who saves his people from their sins. God promised that he himself would redeem his people from all their sins (Ps. 130:8). The baby born in Bethlehem is God incarnate, our Savior, ready to save. That is why the angel told the shepherds that the Savior had come.

When the angel delivered the Lord's message to Mary and Joseph about the child Mary would bear, the name of this infant was not left for the parents to determine arbitrarily. God himself chose the name, which revealed the mission of this child: *"You are to give him the name Jesus"* (v. 21) or "Joshua," which means "Jehovah saves" or "God saves."

Jesus is the exclusive Savior. In the Greek text of Matthew 1:21, we read that he alone will save his people from their sins. So the angel told Joseph, *"You will call him Jesus because it is he that will save [meaning, he alone will save] his people from their sins."*

No man can save any other man, or even himself, from his sins. It is the God/man, Jesus Christ, alone who can save. As God/man, he lived a perfect life and died a vicarious death for our sins. That is why we say that Jesus alone is the Savior and there is none other. People can believe in any religion they want, but there is no other Savior outside of Christ. The deepest need of all men is for a Savior. That Savior is Jesus. He is God who saves and he is man who died for our sins. Salvation is of the Lord, and Jesus Christ alone is Lord.

Not only is Jesus the God who saves, but he is also the only effectual Savior. *"He will save his people from their sins."* Jesus did not merely make salvation possible; he does save his people, without contingency or uncertainty. There is definiteness, a certainty, in his actions.

Jesus will save all those who are *"his people."* John writes, "For God so loved the world that he gave his one and only Son, that whoever believes in him shall not perish but have everlasting life" (John 3:16). That is true, but Jesus also tells us, "My sheep listen to my voice" (John 10:27). Those who are his people will listen to him. And not only that, Jesus adds, "I know them, and they follow me." So when Jesus calls them, his people will listen, repent, believe, and follow him. If you are not listening to him, believing in him, or following him, it means you are not included in his people and he has no obligation to save you.

Jesus came to save not only Jews but also Gentiles. He said, "I have other sheep that are not of this sheep pen. I must bring them also. They too will listen to my voice, and there shall be one flock and one shepherd" (John 10:16). Here we see that those who are not Jewish can rejoice, for Jesus includes Gentiles as well as Jews in his people.

Who, then, are Jesus' people? They are those whom God the Father donated to the Son to save. God from all eternity gave a certain number of people to the Son to save, and the Son agreed to save them. As we read in Jesus' high priestly prayer, "I have revealed you to those whom you gave me out of the world. They were yours; you gave them to me and they have obeyed your word" (John 17:6). We do not believe in the universalist notion that everyone is going to be saved. But out of the world, God gave a certain number of people to his Son to save. Such people will hear and follow Christ and be saved. This is called definitive salvation or particular redemption.

We see this particularism again when Jesus said, "I pray for them. I am not praying for the world, but for those you have given me, for they are yours" (John 17:9). He also said, "Father, I want those you have given me to be with me where I am" (John 17:24). So God does not save all, but he does save some.

Jesus also declared, "All that the Father gives me will come to me" (John 6:37). "Come to me" here means to put one's faith in Christ. There is a certainty about this statement which shows the effectiveness of this salvation. Jesus continued, "and whoever comes to me I will never drive away." In other words, he was saying, "I will save my people. They will come to me and I will save them."

Jesus also said, "And this is the will of him who sent me, that I shall lose none of all that he has given me, but raise them up at the last day" (John 6:39). Jesus saved his people by his death on the cross. Many people think of Jesus as "sweet Jesus" or "little baby Jesus" and sing lullabies about him. But we must never divorce this infant from the totality of his life's mission and purpose.

Who Is Jesus?

Who, then, is the infant Jesus whose birth we celebrate? He is God, King, and Savior, who came to save his people by his death on the cross. Jesus himself said, "The Son of Man did not come to be served, but to serve, and to give his life as a ransom for many" (Matt. 20:28). We must understand that he saves his people *from* their sins, not *in* their sins or *in spite of* their sins. We are not speaking about a salvation from physical danger or disease or poverty or a political condition, but a comprehensive salvation. The salvation God gives us through his Son is nothing less than total liberation from the guilt of sin, the pollution of sin, the power of sin, the punishment of sin, and, finally, the presence of sin.

This helpless, homeless, thumb-sucking baby Jesus lying in a manger does not need us or anything else in the universe. But we need him to be our God, our King, and our Savior. We need him to tell us, as he told the paralytic, "Son, your sins are forgiven." We need him to tell us, as he told the sinful woman, "Your sins are forgiven. Go in peace." Jesus alone is our salvation and Savior. He alone is our peace and the Prince of peace. He not only saves us from all our sins, but he also saves us to eternal blessing. He alone can give us eternal life, communion of the Holy Spirit, and peace with God. As Paul writes, "Therefore, since we have been justified through faith, we have peace with God through our Lord Jesus Christ" (Rom. 5:1). The infant born in Bethlehem accomplished all of this.

When Jesus was born, no one of earthly importance or stature came to celebrate his birth. But the heavenly host of angels sang for his birthday, "Glory to God in the highest, and on earth peace to men on whom his favor rests" (Luke 2:14). In the same way, we also can sing, "Glory to God for his justice! Glory to God for his mercy! Glory to God for the gift of his Son, who accomplished peace on earth!" As we read in Isaiah 9:2, "The people walking in darkness have seen a great light; on those living in the land of the shadow of death a light has dawned."

This God, this Son, this King, this Savior, this Christ will liberate us from the iron chains of sin—not from some abstract, theoretical sins, but from real sins. As a result, those who are thieves will become earners and givers; those who are idolaters will become true worshipers of the living God; those who are adulterers will become faithful husbands and wives; those who are liars will become truth-tellers; and those who are drunkards will become sober. This is the real freedom Christ brings to his people.

Zechariah saw this infant Jesus as the rising sun coming to us from heaven "to shine on those living in darkness and in the shadow of death, to guide our feet into the path of peace" (Luke 1:78–79). He is the light of the world who makes us also the light of the world in him.

We must never feel sorry for Jesus or think that we can do him any favors. I know many people only show up in the church on Easter and on Christmas. They think that God must appreciate the effort they make to come. I hope such people will realize that instead of them coming on their own efforts, God himself is bringing them because he loves them and wants them to hear the gospel and be saved. It is this same God who made his salvation so simple, saying, "Everyone who comes to me I will save."

Do not feel sorry for this infant Jesus. Do not weep for him, as he said to the women on his way to be crucified. Instead, recognize that this infant is the true God, the King of kings and Lord of lords, and the only Savior. Is he your God, King, and Savior? You may only have a few Christmases left. Have you repented of your sins and trusted in Christ alone for your salvation? Have you owned him as God, as King, as Savior? Have you joined the angels in singing, "Glory to God in the highest"?

The shepherds joined in the singing. Later on, Simeon and Anna also joined in the singing. In heaven we find even more people singing. John writes,

> After this I looked and there before me was a great multitude that no one could count, from every nation, tribe, people and language, standing before the throne and in front of the Lamb. They were wearing white robes and were holding palm branches in their hands. And they cried out in a loud voice: "Salvation belongs to our God, who sits on the throne, and to the Lamb." All the angels were standing around the throne and around the elders and the four living creatures. They fell down on their faces before the throne and worshiped God, saying: "Amen! Praise and glory and wisdom and thanks and honor and power and strength be to our God for ever and ever. Amen!" (Rev. 7:9–12)

May God help us to see this Jesus not as a mere man but as he truly is, the only God, King, and Savior. May we believe in him so that we may sing his praises both now and throughout eternity.

6
Good News of Mega Joy

MATTHEW 1:18–25

This is how the birth of Jesus Christ came about: His mother Mary was pledged to be married to Joseph, but before they came together, she was found to be with child through the Holy Spirit.

Matthew 1:18

The Audacity of Hope by President Barack Obama was about having a bold, arrogant hope in man. It does not speak about our hope, which is in our Savior, Christ the Lord, born in Bethlehem about two thousand years ago.

All hope that is based in sinful, dying men is worthless. Paul says, "If only for this life we have hope in Christ, we are to be pitied more than all men" (1 Cor. 15:19). Sinful man's help is worthless (Ps. 60:11). Sinful man's hope is only in this world, and his hope is truly hopelessness.

John tells us, "Love not the world, neither the things that are in the world. If any man love the world, the love of the Father is not in him. For all that is in the world, the lust of the flesh, and the lust of the eyes, and the pride of life, is not of the Father, but is of the world," that is, from the devil. "And the world passeth away, and the lust thereof: but he that doeth the will of God abideth for ever" (1 John 2:15–17, KJV). Remember what Jesus said: "What does it profit if you gain the whole world yet lose your soul?" (Mark 8:36).

My hope is not in man or in this world. So I sing,

My hope is built on nothing less
than Jesus' blood and righteousness.

I dare not trust the sweetest frame
but wholly lean on Jesus' name.
On Christ the solid rock I stand;
all other ground is sinking sand,
all other ground is sinking sand.

The Audacity of Hope is other ground. It is sinking sand that saves no one. In fact, such "hope" makes human beings wicked, arrogant, and stubborn. Such people refuse to trust in Jesus Christ alone for their eternal salvation.

Sinful men are without hope and without God in this world (Eph. 2:12). God appointed man once to die and then face God's judgment (Heb. 9:27). The psalmist counsels us, "O Israel, put your hope in the LORD, for with the LORD is unfailing love and with him is full redemption. He himself will redeem Israel from all their sins" (Ps. 130:7–8).

In Christ alone, we have living hope (1 Pet. 1:3). Man trusts in his puny intellect, in his money, in his fading beauty, in his power, and in his pedigree. But all must die.

The angel spoke to virgin Mary, to Joseph, and to the poor shepherds of Bethlehem about Jesus: "To you today I bring good news of great joy" (Luke 2:10–11). In the fullness of time a Savior was born; he is Christ the Lord. He is not a sinful man pretending to save sinful men. He is very God and very man, who, by his atoning death and resurrection, will save all who repent and believe in him alone. He is the only Savior of the whole world. He is the hope of glory. Only in Jesus do we have the hope of eternal life.

Joseph's Dilemma

In Matthew 1:18–25, Matthew records the virgin birth of Christ. In the incarnation, the Holy Spirit begat and the virgin Mary conceived without the agency of a man. This was miraculous in three ways: It was supernatural begetting; the person begat was supernatural; and he was supernaturally preserved, so that Jesus was born sinless, unlike Mary and any other human being.[14]

---

14 John Murray, *Collected Writings*, vol. 2, *Systematic Theology* (Edinburgh: Banner of Truth, 1977), 134–135.

Matthew tells us that Mary was pledged to be married to Joseph (Matt. 1:18). This betrothal created a legal state of marriage. But before they began to live together, which usually took place after a year, it was reported to Joseph that Mary was found to be with a child in her womb. This pregnancy came about *ek pneumatos hagiou* (by the Holy Ghost).

The Bible testifies to this miraculous conception in several places (Matt. 1:18, 20, 23; Luke 1:27, 31, 34, 35). It was also prophesied by Isaiah (Isa. 7:14). Matthew states clearly that Mary's supernatural virginal conception was the fulfillment of the Isaianic prophecy given seven hundred years earlier. It is very credible that God performs miracles. Luke 1:37 states that there is nothing impossible for God.

Thus, Joseph came to know about this pregnancy of his wife. Perhaps Mary herself reported to him through an intermediary. It is possible that she also told Joseph that it was through the power of the Holy Spirit that she had conceived. But Joseph did not believe the story. Being a righteous, law-abiding man, Joseph refused to take her as his wife. He went to bed planning to divorce her privately by giving her a bill of divorcement.

God's Solution

As we read in Luke 1:38, Mary trusted God to work out this problem. And in the night, while Joseph was sleeping, God's angel appeared to him. He told Joseph that Mary's conception was virginal by the power of the Holy Spirit. He reassured Joseph that Mary was holy, that she had not violated the seventh commandment, and, therefore, Joseph should not be afraid to take Mary home from her father's house. Joseph was overjoyed to hear this message from God.

The angel was probably Gabriel, who had previously appeared to Mary. Now he addressed Joseph, calling him *"son of David,"* because he was an heir to the throne of David (v. 20). The angel commanded Joseph to do a number of things: He was to take Mary home as his wife in domestic union, and he was to provide for her, protect her, guide her, comfort her, and encourage her. He was also told that Mary would give birth to a son, and Joseph was to adopt him by giving him the God-given name of Jesus.

The Precious Name of Jesus

John Murray says Jesus is a precious name. It is used one hundred and fifty times in Matthew's gospel alone. It was not given arbitrarily. God chose and revealed this name to Joseph. It is full of spiritual meaning. "Jesus" is a variant of "Joshua" (or "Jehoshua"), which means "Jehovah [God] saves." It comes from the Hebrew word *yasha*, which means "to save."

The Old Testament says that only God is the Savior: "I, even I, am the LORD, and apart from me there is no savior" (Isa. 43:11). In Hosea 13:4 we read, "But I am the LORD your God. . . . You shall acknowledge no God but me, no Savior except me." Peter identifies this Savior as Jesus: "Salvation is found in no one else, for there is no other name under heaven given to men by which we must be saved" (Acts 4:12)

All other religions are creations of sinful human beings. They cannot save anyone. Only Jesus Christ saves. Have you trusted in Jesus alone for your eternal salvation?

Consider this logic: The Old Testament tells us that God alone saves. But the New Testament tells us that Jesus saves. Therefore, we can make the conclusion that Jesus is God who saves. In the same way, we know from the Old Testament that God alone forgives our sins. But in the New Testament we are told that Jesus forgives our sins. Therefore Jesus is God who forgives sins.

Jesus' name is an exclusive name. In Matthew 1:21 we read that he *alone* (the Greek word *autos* conveys this meaning) saves. There is no other savior. Jesus is the only Savior of the whole world. He will save his people totally. He saves our bodies and our souls.

The Elect of God

In Jesus, therefore, the promise God gave to Abraham was fulfilled, that all the families of the earth would be blessed in him (Gen. 12:3). Jesus is the seed of the woman (the virgin Mary), and he alone would crush the head of the serpent, as promised in Genesis 3:15. He destroyed death, which is the wages of our sin, by his atoning death, and now gives us eternal life.

Jesus destroys our hell and brings us to God in heaven. He saves his people, all the elect, whose names are already written in the Lamb's book of life. He will save all whom the Father gives him, all who are chosen in him and are given grace in him. He saves not only Jews but also Gentiles. So we read, "For those God foreknew he also predestined to be conformed to the likeness of his Son, that he might be the firstborn among many brothers. And those he predestined, he also called; those he called, he also justified; those he justified, he also glorified" (Rom. 8:29–30).

Jesus prayed, "For you granted [the Son] authority over all people that he might give eternal life to all those you have given him. . . . I pray for them. I am not praying for the world." In other words, Jesus was not praying for the vast majority of the people in the world. But the *ekklēsia*, the church, consists of those who are "called out" from the world. So Jesus said, "I pray for them. I am not praying for the world, but for those you have given me, for they are yours" (John 17:2, 9).

Paul writes, "[God] has saved us and called us to a holy life—not because of anything we have done but because of his own purpose and grace. This grace was given us in Christ Jesus before the beginning of time, but it has now been revealed through the appearing of our Savior, Christ Jesus, who has destroyed death and has brought life and immortality to light through the gospel" (2 Tim. 1:9–10). He also says, "But we ought always to thank God for you, brothers loved by the Lord, because from the beginning God chose you to be saved through the sanctifying work of the Spirit and through belief in the truth. He called you to this through our gospel, that you might share in the glory of our Lord Jesus Christ" (2 Thess. 2:13–14).

Jesus saved the despised shepherds, the lowest of the low. He saved the publicans, the prodigals, and the prostitutes. He saved the chief of sinners, as Paul called himself: "Here is a trustworthy saying that deserves full acceptance: Christ Jesus came into the world to save sinners—of whom I am the worst. But for that very reason I was shown mercy so that in me, the worst of sinners, Christ Jesus might display his unlimited patience as an example for those who would believe on him and receive eternal life" (1 Tim. 1:15–16). And Jesus saves us.

God mocks and laughs at the mighty, the audacious, the wicked, the arrogant, the rich, the famous, the intellectuals, the philosophers. If you are not convinced, consider Paul's words: "Brothers, think of what you were when you were called. Not many of you were wise by human standards; not many were influential; not many were of noble birth. But God chose the foolish things of the world to shame the wise." God chose the "foolish" things of the world for the purpose of shaming the wise, the intellectuals, the mighty, the philosophers, the politicians, and so on. Paul continues, "God chose the weak things of the world to shame the strong. He chose the lowly things of this world and the despised things—and the things that are not—to nullify the things that are, so that no one may boast before him" (1 Cor. 1:26–29).

Mary herself had to be saved by her son, the God/man. She confessed that she was a sinner needing a savior: "My soul glorifies the Lord and my spirit rejoices in God my Savior" (Luke 1:46–47). Mary was a sinner just like us; thus, worship of Mary is idolatry. The idea of her immaculate conception is false. Like us, Mary was conceived in sin and born a sinner, and the Messiah, her son Jesus, saved her.

Jesus Saves from Sin

Jesus alone saves his people from their sins. We are not saved in our sins, nor in spite of our sins, but from our sins. If you are living in sin, be warned: You are not a Christian. Jesus saves us away from our sins and makes us more like him. He justifies the ungodly to make them godly. If a person is not living a holy life, he is not a Christian. His name is Jesus, *"because he will save his people from their sins"* (v. 21).

Jesus saves his people from the penalty of sin, which is eternal death, from the power of sin, from the pollution of sin, and even from the presence of sin. Through Christ, his people are saved, they are being saved, and they will be saved in soul and body. It is he who will bring us to glory, both in our bodies and our souls. We are objects of God's mercy prepared for glory, which is the heavenly happiness of the eternal beatific vision.

Jesus will save every one of his people. Jesus said, "This is the will of him who sent me, that I shall lose none of all that he has given me, but raise them up at the last day. For my Father's will is that everyone who looks to the Son and believes in him shall have eternal life, and I will raise him up at the last day" (John 6:39–40).

Jesus will save his people from their sins and bring them to God. He will save them from the root of sin and its fruits, from their evil hearts and evil actions. Our hearts are the problem. Jeremiah says, "The heart is deceitful above all things and beyond cure. Who can understand it?" (Jer. 17:9). Jesus said, "The things that come out of the mouth come from the heart, and these make a man 'unclean.' For out of the heart come evil thoughts, murder, adultery, sexual immorality, theft, false testimony, slander. These are what make a man 'unclean'" (Matt. 15:18–20). Paul writes, "Do you not know that the wicked will not inherit the kingdom of God? Do not be deceived: Neither the sexually immoral nor idolaters nor adulterers nor male prostitutes nor homosexual offenders nor thieves nor the greedy nor drunkards nor slanderers nor swindlers will inherit the kingdom of God. And that is what some of you were. But you were washed, you were sanctified, you were justified in the name of the Lord Jesus Christ and by the Spirit of our God" (1 Cor. 6:9–11). So we read, "The fruit of the Spirit is love, joy, peace, patience, kindness, goodness, faithfulness, gentleness and self-control" (Gal. 5:22–23).

Friends, salvation from sin is not found in anyone else under heaven. No one comes to the Father except through Jesus. There is no way for us to be saved except by faith in Christ and serving him all our lives.

Who Is Jesus?

Do you want to know who Jesus is? He is Immanuel, God with us. He is the only Savior of the whole world. He is the Messiah, the anointed Prophet, Priest and King promised in the Old Testament. He is the Lord, Jehovah God. He is our Wonderful Counselor who alone counsels us from his holy Scriptures. He is the Mighty God of creation, providence, and redemption. He is the Everlasting Father, the Father who cares for us from all eternity and to eternity. He is the Prince of Peace; through him we have peace with God, and because of him, the peace of God comes to our hearts to guard our hearts and minds in Christ Jesus. He is the Son of the Most High, the one and only Son, and in him we are all adopted as sons. We belonged to the family of the devil, but God adopted us and made us sons of God in Jesus. And he is the Good Shepherd who gave his life for the sheep in his substitutionary and propitiatory death on the cross: "He was delivered over to death for our sins and was raised to life for our justification" (Rom. 4:25). We have all sinned, and we all must die. But Jesus died in our place, so instead of death, we have been given eternal life. Our sins have been forgiven forever.

Paul writes, "God [reconciled] the world to himself in Christ, not counting men's sins against them. . . . God made him who had no sin to be sin for us, so that in him we might become the righteousness of God" (2 Cor. 5:19, 21). We are clothed in an alien righteousness, which is the righteousness of God himself.

Joseph believed and obeyed God's instruction. He believed that the miracle of the virginal conception of Mary was by the Holy Spirit. He took her to his home to provide for her, protect her, guide her, comfort her, and serve her. He adopted her son by naming him Jesus, so that he would inherit David's throne forever. By his faith in Christ, Joseph was also saved from his sins.

Believe and Be Saved

What about you? You have heard the gospel. But have you bowed your knees to Christ and confessed him as your Lord? If not, all the hearing of preaching will only contribute to your increased judgment. The Lord Jesus Christ is King of kings forever. If you submit to him and his rule, he will save you.

The shepherds believed and were saved. Joseph and Mary believed and were saved. A vast multitude of people have believed and been saved by this heaven-sent Savior, Jesus Christ the Lord. And thank God, Jesus saved me also. Paul writes, "Therefore, since we have been justified through faith, we have peace with God through our Lord Jesus Christ" (Rom. 5:1). He also says, "Therefore, there is now no condemnation for those who are in Christ Jesus" (Rom. 8:1). Finally, Paul declares,

> What, then, shall we say in response to this? If God is for us, who can be against us? He who did not spare his own Son,

but gave him up for us all—how will he not also, along with him, graciously give us all things? Who will bring any charge against those whom God has chosen? It is God who justifies. Who is he that condemns? Christ Jesus, who died—more than that, who was raised to life—is at the right hand of God and is also interceding for us. Who shall separate us from the love of Christ? Shall trouble or hardship or persecution or famine or nakedness or danger or sword? As it is written: "For your sake we face death all day long; we are considered as sheep to be slaughtered." No, in all these things we are more than conquerors through him who loved us. For I am convinced that neither death nor life, neither angels nor demons, neither the present nor the future, nor any powers, neither height nor depth, nor anything else in all creation, will be able to separate us from the love of God that is in Christ Jesus our Lord. (Rom. 8:31–39)

If you are outside of Christ, he can save you too. He can do so now. The Bible says, "Now is the time of God's favor, now is the day of salvation" (2 Cor. 6:2). What must we do to be saved? Paul declared, "Believe in the Lord Jesus, and you will be saved" (Acts 16:31). He also said, "If you confess with your mouth, 'Jesus is Lord,' and believe in your heart that God raised him from the dead, you will be saved" (Rom. 10:9). Peter said, "Repent and be baptized, every one of you, in the name of Jesus Christ for the forgiveness of your sins" (Acts 2:38).

So believe, confess, and repent. Then pray to Jesus, knowing that "everyone who calls upon the name of the Lord will be saved" (Acts 2:21). As Peter was walking on the water, he saw the wind and was afraid. Beginning to sink, he cried out, "Lord, save me!" (Matt. 14:30), and Jesus saved him. His name is Jesus, for he will save his people from their sins.

If you trust in him, you will possess eternal life. Jesus said, "I tell you the truth, whoever hears my word and believes him who sent me has eternal life and will not be condemned; he has crossed over from death to life" (John 5:24).

Saved people celebrate and worship God. Therefore, let us celebrate! Let us worship God the Father with the multitude of elect angels and all those who are saved from their sins. Let us celebrate with all his people, both in heaven and on earth, and sing, "Gloria in excelsis Deo! Glory to God in the highest, and on earth peace among all who by grace believe in the Son, Jesus Christ, our Lord!" Let us say with Paul, "Now to the King eternal, immortal, invisible, the only God, be honor and glory for ever and ever. Amen" (1 Tim. 1:17). Let us sing a new song with the twenty-four elders in heaven: "You are worthy to take the scroll and to open its seals, because you were slain, and with your blood you purchased men for God from every tribe and language and people and nation. You have made them to be a kingdom and priests to serve our God, and they will reign on the earth" (Rev. 5:9–10). Hallelujah!

7
The Wise
Worship the King

MATTHEW 2:1–12

¹After Jesus was born in Bethlehem in Judea, during the time of King Herod, Magi from the east came to Jerusalem ²and asked, "Where is the one who has been born king of the Jews? We saw his star in the east and have come to worship him."

Matthew 2:1–2

What is the message of the gospel of Matthew? The Messiah has come! In Matthew 1, we read the account of the birth of Jesus who is described as the Christ, the Anointed One. He is the promised Messiah and there is no other. Although some people are still waiting for a Messiah, they must realize that the Messiah has come in Jesus Christ, the son of David, the son of Abraham.

From Matthew 1, we learn that Jesus the Messiah was virgin born, meaning he is the Son of God. We also learn that he is the Savior, the one who saves his people from their sins, and that "his people" includes not only Jews but also Gentiles. And, finally, we are told that Jesus is known as Immanuel, which means "God with us."

Looking for the King

In Matthew 2:1–12, we read of people coming to worship Jesus, the Son of David, the newborn king of the Jews. Who were these worshipers? Were they Jews coming out to Bethlehem from nearby

Jerusalem? To our surprise, as we study this chapter, we see that these worshipers were Gentiles from far away, from the east.

The first thing we learn from this passage is that Jesus is to be worshiped by all the peoples of the world. As we have already said, the phrase "his people" includes Gentiles as well as Jews. God's plan is to save people from all nations. We read about this when King Jesus gave the great commission to his disciples: "All authority in heaven and on earth has been given to me. Therefore go and make disciples of all nations, baptizing them in the name of the Father and of the Son and of the Holy Spirit, and teaching them to obey everything I have commanded you. And surely I am with you always, to the very end of the age" (Matt. 28:18–20). God calls his people from all nations; therefore, these Gentiles were called to travel from the east to worship their newborn King.

Born in Bethlehem

Matthew begins his second chapter by stating that *"Jesus was born in Bethlehem in Judea"* (v. 1). Why did he include this information? He did so because he was interested in writing a history of the life of Jesus, not in fabricating a legend. Therefore, he tells us exactly where Jesus was born. But why did he specify Bethlehem in Judea? At that time there was also a Bethlehem in Galilee, in the north of Israel. Jesus was born in the Bethlehem in the south, so Matthew wrote "Bethlehem of Judea" for clarity.

What was Bethlehem like at that time? As we noted before, the name Bethlehem means "house of bread." The fertile fields of Bethlehem produced a large amount of grain. Bethlehem itself also functioned as a granary in which large amounts of grain were stored. The grain was made into bread for the nourishment of physical bodies. In God's ordination, Jesus Christ, the living bread who feeds our souls, was born in Bethlehem, the house of bread.

Bethlehem is about five miles south of Jerusalem. It was in Bethlehem that Jacob buried his favorite wife Rachel after she died in childbirth. It was also in Bethlehem that Boaz tended his grain fields and met and married Ruth, from whom was descended David. In Bethlehem, David was born, and it was for the cool waters from the well of Bethlehem that David expressed longing in 2 Samuel 23:15. And in the fullness of time, Jesus

Christ, the living water who quenches the spiritual thirst of all people, was also born in Bethlehem.

The little town of Bethlehem was destined for glory, and that glory came to it through the birth of the son of David, Jesus Christ the Messiah. This was not a surprise to Jewish scholars who studied the Scriptures diligently. Seven hundred years before the birth of Christ, God spoke through the prophet Micah that the shepherd of Israel, the ruler, would come out of Bethlehem in the land of Judea (Mic. 5:2). Thus, it was Jesus who gave glory to Bethlehem. In the same way, he makes glorious everyone who makes room for him.

During the Time of Herod

In his desire to create an accurate historical record, Matthew also recorded the time Jesus was born: *"Jesus was born in Bethlehem in Judea, during the time of King Herod"* (v. 1). Christianity is based on a historical account, not on a legend. Its foundation is in events that occurred in space and time.

"King Herod" refers to Herod the Great. We can call him Herod the great fox, because Jesus called his son, Herod Antipas, a fox (Luke 13:32). Herod the Great was the father of Herod Antipas, who interacted with Jesus, as well as the father of Herod Philip I, Herod Philip II, and Archelaus, a brutal king who ruled Judea from 4 BC to AD 6.

Herod the Great was an Edomite, not a Jew. He was the son of Antipater and his Arab wife. Herod was born in 73 BC and died in 4 BC. He began to rule in 40 BC when the Roman senate gave him power to do so. Eventually, he became the king of all of Palestine. He was wealthy, gifted, cruel, capable, and crafty. He was a shrewd politician and a great builder. In 20 BC, Herod began to rebuild the second temple, a project that was finished sixty-eight years after his death. Despite Herod's interest in rebuilding the temple, he was resented by the Jews because he was an Edomite and a usurper.

Herod was a shrewd politician who wanted to hold on to power. He would kill anyone who posed a threat to his position, whether the threat was real or imaginary. He killed his wife, Mariamne; his mother-in-law, Alexandra; his oldest son, Antipater;

and two other sons, Alexander and Aristobulus. He killed his brother-in-law, his uncle, and thousands of others to ensure that he and he alone would be the king of Palestine. He killed the male babies of Bethlehem, as we also read about in Matthew 2. In fact, Herod decreed in his will that on the day he died his friends should arrest leading citizens of Palestine on trumped up charges and murder them. Why? He wanted great mourning in the land when he died, and he knew no one would shed a tear for his death.

It was during the reign of King Herod the Great, possibly around 5 BC, that the Magi, the wise men from the east, came to Jerusalem. They asked, *"Where is the one who has been born king of the Jews? We saw his star in the east and have come to worship him"* (v. 2). These Gentiles came at this time for the singular purpose of worshiping the newborn Christ.

Some Wise Men Seek Him

The Magi were members of the priestly class of Persia, or Babylon. They were educated in philosophy, medicine, general science, and dream interpretation. They were the wise men, the soothsayers of their time.

The Bible speaks about wise men of Egypt and Babylon and portrays them as objects of mocking. Although they were continually called on by their rulers to interpret what the God of Israel was doing, they always failed to do so. Wise men failed Pharaoh, Nebuchadnezzar, and Belshazzar. The Bible mocks at their total inability to discern the times and interpret what God was saying.

Yet it seems that some of these wise men, the Magi, had a desire to know the truth about the God of Israel and to search for that truth. Perhaps they were aided in their search by their contact with the Jewish community in the Diaspora in the east. This passage in Matthew 2 shows us that God had chosen the wise men, these Gentiles from the east, to know the truth. He supernaturally guided them to come to Israel to worship Jesus, the Savior of the world, the only source of truth.

We can rejoice in God's choosing these wise men to know him. No man, wise or not, will, on his own, desire to know the true and living God. God spoke through the apostle Paul about the wise people of the world and what they do: "For it is written: 'I will destroy the wisdom of the wise; the intelligence of the intelligent I will frustrate.' Where is the wise man? Where is the scholar? Where is the philosopher of this age? Has not God made foolish the wisdom of the world? For since in the wisdom of God the world through its wisdom did not know him, God was pleased through the foolishness of what was preached to save those who believe" (1 Cor. 1:19–21). He also said, "Brothers, think of what you were when you were called. Not many of you were wise by human standards" (1 Cor. 1:26).

Not many wise men will come to know God. But we must note with great joy that Paul did not say "not any"; he said "not many." Here we find that God did choose some wise people, these Magi, the intellectuals of their time, to seek after him.

As those chosen of God from all eternity to worship Christ, these wise men were given a desire to worship the newborn king of the Jews. And God enabled them to travel hundreds of miles, making a long and arduous journey that probably took about a year. They spent much time, money, and energy on their quest to find the Christ.

God gave the wise men a supernatural guidance system to lead them to the newborn king. The same God who had guided Israel during the exodus from Egypt through the wilderness and into the land of promise by a pillar of fire and a pillar of cloud now guided these Gentiles to Jesus Christ, the King of the Jews, by a star.

What was this mysterious star? I agree with those who say that all attempts to explain the star as a natural phenomenon are inadequate and a waste of time. Matthew 2:9 says that the star that went before them stood right over the house of Joseph, Mary, and Jesus. A conjunction of planets, a supernova, a comet, or a UFO are all inadequate reasons for such an occurrence. This star was a supernatural guidance system, a luminary from God which hung low in the sky and moved ahead of the Magi, leading them first to Jerusalem, then to Bethlehem and, finally, to the house of King Jesus.

The Magi were true wise men, not frauds and charlatans like the wise men we read about in other portions of Scripture. How can I say they were wise? These men believed in the revelation of Scripture regarding the King of the Jews and went to great pains to find and worship him. They feared God. "The fear of the LORD is the beginning of wisdom, and knowledge of the Holy One is understanding" (Prov. 9:10).

True wise men will fear and worship the King of kings. We read about this in Psalm 2:10–12: "Therefore, you kings, be wise; be warned, you rulers of the earth. Serve the LORD with fear and rejoice with trembling. Kiss the Son, lest he be angry and you be destroyed in your way, for his wrath can flare up in a moment. Blessed are all who take refuge in him."

These wise men feared the Lord. So they traveled all the way from their homes to Jerusalem to inquire about the newborn king. They probably should have continued past Jerusalem, following the star to Bethlehem, but possibly they stopped because they thought the King of the Jews would be found in a major city. And while they were in Jerusalem, Herod heard of their quest. They asked, *"Where is the one who has been born king of the Jews? We saw his star in the east and have come to worship him"* (v. 2).

These wise men were really missionaries from the east to the west. What was the news they brought to the city of Jerusalem? "Your king is born! We heard the King of the Jews was born, and though we are Gentiles, we want to worship him. In fact, we came from far away to do so. Where, then, is the King of the Jews?"

The Magi were announcing that the messianic expectations of the Jews had now been fulfilled in the birth of Christ. No more waiting was necessary. This was the time to rejoice! This was the time spoken about in Isaiah 52:7: "How beautiful on the mountains are the feet of those who bring good news, who proclaim peace, who bring good tidings, who proclaim salvation, who say to Zion, 'Your God reigns!'"

Were the Jews saying anything about the infant Jesus? No. God chose some wise men from the east and guided them all the way to Jerusalem to tell the people of Zion, "Your king is born!" Through these wise men the good news of the gospel was brought to the Jews, to the city of Jerusalem, to the rulers of Jerusalem, and to the scholars of Jerusalem. What was their gospel? "Rejoice, O Zion! Your king—the king you were expecting, the king who will shepherd you and deliver you and comfort you and give you peace—has been born! The days of oppression are gone and the days of salvation are here. Rejoice!"

Reactions to the Good News

How did the people of Jerusalem react to these missionaries? First, let us look at Herod. The Bible says he was disturbed and upset when he heard these things. In fact, we read that all Jerusalem was disturbed with him (v. 3). Why was this? The people of Jerusalem were disturbed because they knew that when cruel King Herod was distressed, he could do many destructive things. So, as the citizens of Jerusalem trembled, Herod gathered together the Jewish scholars, the Sanhedrin, and asked them, "Tell me, where is the Christ going to be born?" And having studied these things for many years, they readily answered, "Bethlehem of Judea," five miles south of Jerusalem.

After talking to the scholars, Herod met secretly with the wise men and asked them exactly when they first saw the star. Then he instructed them to go to Bethlehem and make a diligent search for the king, find him, and report back to Herod so that he could worship him also. But ruthless Herod did not really intend to worship Christ. He wanted to kill him. He is similar to people who come to church and say they want to worship. They might stand up and say, "I received Jesus Christ," and make vows, but, like Herod, they have another agenda.

We are not surprised that Herod was disturbed at the news of Jesus' birth. Christ the King comes to disturb and upset us. He disturbs our own comfort so that we can receive his comfort. But how should we react? Should we try to kill Jesus, as Herod did? No. We must fall prostrate before him. When King Jesus comes, we must repent and say goodbye to all ideas that are not centered on him. That is what repentance means. We must humble ourselves. We must decrease, and he must increase. He alone is Lord, King, and Christ. He alone is God with us, and we must recognize him as such.

Worship or kill. There are only two reactions to Christ. Herod refused to kiss the Son, so he planned to eliminate him. Herod would not tolerate competition, real or perceived. But what about us? Do not some of us do the same thing? Why do you think some people do not want to believe in Jesus? Because they cannot tolerate competition. But he alone is Lord. Everyone else must humble themselves and adore him.

Herod was the seed of the serpent that we read about in Genesis 3. He would not submit to Christ and worship him. But God was not afraid of Herod. Salvation is of divine plan and purpose, and God alone is sovereign. What he purposes, he performs, and no one can thwart his plan. He does all things according to the counsel of his own will. Nations, kingdoms, and armies are nothing before him. Human power, the power of a Pharaoh or a Nebuchadnezzar, let alone a little Idumean king Herod, is nothing before him. All men are mist, vapor, and grass.

Soon after the birth of Christ, Herod died a wretched death and entered into an eternal destiny of distress. Why? He refused to believe in Jesus and worship him.

How did the Sanhedrin react to the news of the wise men that Jesus was born? The members of the Sanhedrin were great scholars who diligently studied the Scriptures. When Herod asked them where the Messiah would be born, they instantly gave the correct answer based on their understanding of the Scriptures. Surely Herod was impressed by their great knowledge.

But the orthodoxy of these professional scholars did not save them. They had no real interest in the newborn King of the Jews. They earned their living by discussing theology in a theoretical way, but they had no use for Christ. They knew the wise men of the east had traveled a long way to Israel, guided supernaturally by a star. But they would not go with them even five miles to Bethlehem to worship the King that the wise men had traveled so far to see. They refused to believe in the gospel message brought to them by these Gentiles. They would not repent and humble themselves. They would not fall down and worship. They also would not kiss the Son. Like Herod, they were destined for destruction. Their unbelief and indifference proved their miserable destiny.

In Matthew 19 and 20, Jesus says twice that the first shall be last and the last shall be first. This is the biblical order. Herod the king and the Jewish scholars, those who had all the benefits of Israel, were last.

Jesus came to his own people, "but his own did not receive him" (John 1:11). Yes, these scholars had searched and studied the Scriptures diligently. But they missed the clear message of the Bible, that God would send a Messiah: Jesus, the son of David, the son of Abraham, the son of God; Jesus, who is Immanuel, the Savior of the world; Jesus, who saves his people from their sins.

Jesus spoke about his unbelieving generation: "The men of Nineveh will stand up at the judgment with this generation and condemn it . . ." The men of Nineveh were Gentiles, but, notice, "for they repented at the preaching of Jonah, and now one greater than Jonah is here. The Queen of the South will rise at the judgment with this generation and condemn it; for she came from the ends of the earth to listen to Solomon's wisdom, and now one greater than Solomon is here" (Matt. 12:41–42). The wise men of the east came all the way to worship him who is wiser than all.

The Wise Worship the King

Finally, the Magi reached the end of their long journey. The star guided them to the place where Jesus, Joseph, and Mary lived. God did not need the Sanhedrin to guide the Magi. They began their trip with the star and ended it with the star. The star stopped over the home of the newborn King, which was now a house, not a cave.

Matthew writes, *"On coming to the house, they saw the child with his mother Mary, and they bowed down and worshiped him"* (v. 11). Notice, the child is mentioned first. He is the one who is emphasized. What did the wise men do when they came in? They fell face down before this child in worship.

How do we react when we meet Jesus? Many of us do not want to fall down. We want to sit on our thrones and rule until the wrath of this One flares up. We do not want him to upset or disturb us. We are like Caiaphas, who also did not want to be disturbed by Jesus. What was Caiaphas' solution? "Let's eliminate him," he said.

But these Gentiles from the east went into the house, fell down, and worshiped Jesus. Notice, they did not worship Mary. Mary herself must worship Jesus. He alone is the King, the Savior, the Christ. He alone is Immanuel, the Son of God. He alone is to be worshiped.

Not only did the Magi fall down in worship and adoration, but they also gave gifts to the child. This was genuine worship. It had already cost them much. They had endured a long journey, suffered along the way, and lost one year of time. But the wise men loved this King of the Jews so much that now, in addition to what they had already given in terms of time and effort, they joyfully presented him with gifts that had also cost them much: gold and frankincense. These gifts were fit for a king who is God. And they also gave him myrrh, fit for the one who was destined to suffer and die.

Genuine worship is costly. Remember what David said when he was given a chance to sacrifice to God without spending any money: "I will not sacrifice to the LORD my God burnt offerings that cost me nothing" (2 Sam. 24:24). David was saying that he would not sacrifice unless it cost him something—not to buy his salvation, but in thankfulness to God for saving him.

In John 12, we read about Mary, the sister of Lazarus and Martha, who sat at the feet of Jesus and believed in him as her Savior. During a dinner given for Jesus, she came with a pint of pure nard, an expensive perfume, broke the bottle, and poured it all on the feet of Jesus. This is costly worship. Those who worship Jesus delight to give to him extravagantly in thankfulness for their salvation.

The wise men came seeking him who was born King of the Jews and Savior of the world. They met him, worshiped him, and loved him. And in so doing, these Gentiles joined the company of Mary, Joseph, Simeon, Anna, the shepherds, and other Jewish believers. They sought, they found, and they were glad.

The Destiny of Fools and the Destiny of the Wise

What are you seeking with all your heart? Most people are seeking money, fame, power, and pleasure. In this country, most people are committed to the pursuit of happiness and most are trying to achieve it one way or another. But Jesus Christ, this one who was born King of the Jews, told his disciples to seek first the kingdom of God and his righteousness.

Are you like Herod, desiring to stay in power no matter what, and eliminating everyone you can, including Jesus, if possible?

If so, you will die a wretched death and enter into an eternity of distress. Are you like the scribes, always studying the Bible, always talking about theology, yet completely indifferent to the greatest news ever told and not even traveling five miles to find out if it is true? This is hardheartedness.

What was the end of these people? As we said, Herod died and entered into his destiny of eternal distress. The scribes experienced the same. They thought they were wise and powerful, but they were fools. Fools have no fear of God before their eyes.

What are you seeking? Do you realize that the King of the Jews has been born? Salvation is of the Jews, and in this King all the families of the earth will be blessed. Not only has he been born, but he also died for our sins and rose for our justification. Let us get up from our thrones, join the wise men of the east, fall down, and worship Christ. "O come, let us adore him!"

What if you cannot bring expensive gold, frankincense or myrrh? It does not matter. God owns it all already and he gives us all things. You must realize that salvation is rich and free. As John Newton wrote, "Amazing grace, how sweet the sound, that saved a wretch like me!" You may not be able to bring gold, frankincense, or myrrh to this King, but you can give him your heart as a gift and love him with your whole heart, mind, soul and strength. Kiss this Son and rejoice in his great salvation!

Are you wise? Then fear the Lord, because those who are truly wise will worship the King of kings and Lord of lords. The day of the Lord is coming soon and on that day "every knee shall bow . . . and every tongue confess that Jesus Christ is Lord, to the glory of God the Father" (Phil. 2:10–11). I urge you to bow your knees now, and you will be saved.

8
Mary's Magnificat
LUKE 1:46-55

⁴⁶And Mary said: "My soul glorifies the Lord ⁴⁷and my spirit rejoices in God my Savior, ⁴⁸for he has been mindful of the humble state of his servant. From now on all generations will call me blessed, ⁴⁹for the Mighty One has done great things for me—holy is his name. ⁵⁰His mercy extends to those who fear him, from generation to generation. ⁵¹He has performed mighty deeds with his arm; he has scattered those who are proud in their inmost thoughts. ⁵²He has brought down rulers from their thrones but has lifted up the humble. ⁵³He has filled the hungry with good things but has sent the rich away empty. ⁵⁴He has helped his servant Israel, remembering to be merciful ⁵⁵to Abraham and his descendants forever, even as he said to our fathers."

Luke 1:46-55

In Luke 1:46–55, we find the portion of Scripture called "Mary's Magnificat." This great worship hymn of Mary is called the Magnificat because it begins in the Latin Bible with the words "*Magnificat anima mea Dominum*," which means "My soul magnifies the Lord."

The gospel of Luke is filled with music, especially the first two chapters. There we find five hymns: the hymn of Elizabeth (Luke 1:42–45); the hymn of Mary (Luke 1:46–55); the hymn of Zechariah (Luke 1:68–79); the hymn of the angels, "Glory to God in the highest, and on earth peace to men on whom his favor rests" (Luke 2:14); and the hymn of Simeon (Luke 2:29–32), which he prayed when he saw the infant Jesus Christ and realized that God's promise that he would not die until he saw God's salvation had just been fulfilled.

Context

The Christmas season is a time of great singing and joy because of the divine announcement of good news of great joy to all the people of the world. As sinners, we need a divine Savior, and the message of Christmas is that God has given us such a competent Savior in his Son who became man, the Lord Jesus Christ.

This divine announcement first came to a poor Jewish teenager, a peasant girl who lived in the despised town of Nazareth in northern Israel. The divine Savior made his grand entrance into history by being born, not in the famous cities of Rome or Jerusalem, but in Bethlehem; not to a famous queen mother, but to a poor Jewish teenager betrothed to the town carpenter; not in a palace, but in a stable, and then placed in a manger.

The angel Gabriel told Mary that by the power of the Holy Spirit she would conceive and give birth to a son who would be the Holy One, the Son of God, the Son of the Most High, the King of Israel, heir to the throne of David. Mary and Joseph were to call him Jesus, for he would save his people from their sins.

Mary was puzzled at this stupendous announcement the angel made to her. "How will this be," she asked the angel, "since I am a virgin?" (Luke 1:34). In other words, "How can a virgin conceive without the aid of a man?" Mary knew that the recent miracle of her elderly relative Elizabeth conceiving was not unique, because such a miracle had happened previously when God enabled Sarah to conceive Isaac. But for a virgin to conceive and give birth to a son was unique, so Mary asked the angel, "How will this be?"

"The Holy Spirit will do it," Gabriel told Mary. "The Holy Spirit will come upon you, and the power of the Most High will overshadow you" (Luke 1:35). Then he added, "For nothing is impossible with God" (Luke 1:37).

Nothing is impossible with God! We must keep this in mind always. How did the universe come to be? The answer is God. How are we going to be raised from the dead? The answer, again, is God. How could Zechariah and barren Elizabeth have a son in their old age through natural human reproductive processes? The answer is God. How could a virgin conceive and give birth to the Savior, Jesus Christ, who is eternal God? The answer is God.

God is sovereign, and he alone does what he pleases. Nothing is impossible for him.

Mary's confusion disappeared at this answer she received from the angel. She told Gabriel, "I am the Lord's servant." Then she said, "May it be to me as you have said." Mary believed God.

Mary's Song

After the angel left, Mary got up quickly and traveled to Judea to visit with Elizabeth, who was six months pregnant. When Elizabeth saw Mary, an amazing thing happened: through the Spirit of the living God, she recognized Mary, this unmarried teenage girl, as "the mother of my Lord," and began to prophesy.

When that happened, Mary also began to sing in the Spirit, exalting and worshiping God. It is this song that is recorded as the Magnificat, and at this point I want to note something: Although Mary was just a poor peasant girl, she had been brought up in a godly home, where she was thoroughly versed in the Scriptures. Like Zechariah, Simeon, Anna, and others, Mary was looking forward to God's redemption of Israel. So when she heard Elizabeth's greeting, she was filled with the Holy Spirit, and scripture came pouring out of her heart.

Let us, then, look at Mary's knowledge of the Lord as she magnifies him. Psalm 103:1 tells us, "Praise the LORD, O my soul; all my inmost being, praise his holy name," and elsewhere we are told that out of the abundance of the heart, our mouths will speak. Mary was filled with God and his grace; thus, she sang about God and his attributes. In this study, we want to examine the seven attributes of God that Mary speaks about in her song.

God Is Mighty

The first attribute Mary speaks of is the might and power of God. He is the mighty One, *ho dunatos*. In Luke 1:49, she sings, *"For the Mighty One has done great things for me."* Mary's God was God Almighty, the Creator of the ends of the earth. There is no one mightier than her God. He alone is able, and with him nothing is impossible.

God himself spoke of this aspect of his character to Abraham in Genesis 18:14, asking, "Is anything too hard for the LORD?" The psalmist says, "Our God is in heaven; he does whatever pleases him" (Ps. 115:3). Jesus himself said, "With man this is impossible, but with God all things are possible" (Matt. 19:26). The apostle Paul recognized this and wrote, "Now to him who is able to do immeasurably more than all we ask or imagine . . ." (Eph. 3:20).

In the first part of verse 51, Mary says of this mighty God, *"He has performed mighty deeds with his arm."* From Genesis 1 on, the Bible speaks of the great and marvelous acts performed by the mighty arm of God. No Pharaoh can resist him. No Sennacherib can defy him. No Nebuchadnezzar can defeat him. No Belshazzar can ignore him. No Caesar can oppose him. Their knees knock when God looks down from his throne. All nations together are considered as nothing by this El-Shaddai, this God, the strong and mighty one. He alone is almighty, and Mary knew it.

Let me ask you: Are you weak? The answer, of course, is yes. But that is not the end. He is strong, and it is in him that we trust. What about the devil and his demons? Are they strong? Yes. Martin Luther recognized that in his great hymn, "A Mighty Fortress," and all of us must recognize it. But our God is stronger than all the forces of this world. Remember what Luther said? "One little Word shall fell him." That Word is the name of Jesus.

Knowing who God is, Mary realized that she had nothing to fear. We too have nothing to fear. The gates of hell cannot prevail against us, because our God is mighty. Thus, we can say with Paul, "We are more than conquerors through him who loved us" (Rom. 8:37).

God Is Holy

The second attribute Mary speaks about is God's holiness. In verse 49, Mary also declares, *"Holy is his name."* Throughout the Scriptures, God tells us, "Be ye holy, for I am holy." God is light, and in him there is no darkness at all. He is the One separate from us—the One without sin.

Isaiah writes of God: "For this is what the high and lofty One says—he who lives forever, whose name is holy: 'I live in a high and holy place'" (Isa. 57:15). In Isaiah 6, the prophet records his reaction when confronted with this holy God:

> In the year that King Uzziah died, I saw the Lord seated on a throne, high and exalted, and the train of his robe filled the temple. Above him were seraphs, each with six wings: With two wings they covered their faces, with two they covered their feet, and with two they were flying. And they were calling to one another: "Holy, holy, holy is the LORD Almighty; the whole earth is full of his glory." At the sound of their voices the doorposts and thresholds shook and the temple was filled with smoke. "Woe to me!" I cried. "I am ruined! For I am a man of unclean lips, and I live among a people of unclean lips, and my eyes have seen the King, the LORD Almighty." (Isa. 6:1–5)

God is not like us. He is just, and, therefore, he must deal with all evil. The wages of sin is eternal death. The Bible tells us the wrath of God is revealed against all ungodliness and unrighteousness of men. Because God is holy, there is judgment and hell.

God Is a Judge

The third attribute Mary speaks about is that God is a judge. In the latter part of Luke 1:51 she says, *"He has scattered those who are proud in their inmost thoughts."* Additionally, in verse 52 we find, *"He has brought down the mighty rulers from their thrones,"* and in verse 53, *"He has sent the rich empty away."*

God scatters those who are arrogant in the thoughts of their hearts. What is the problem with human beings? They are arrogant in their imaginations. What does God do with such people? He scatters these intellectuals who use their minds to oppose God and try to get rid of him. Fallen man always exalts himself above God in his twisted imagination. In Psalm 14 we read, "The fool has said in his heart, 'There is no God.'" The fools of the world hate and revile God, saying, like Pharaoh of old, "Who is the Lord, that we should obey him?" Such people claim to be wise, but, in reality, they are fools, deliberately suppressing the knowledge of God.

The apostle Paul speaks of such fools in 1 Corinthians 1:20, asking, "Where is the wise man? Where is the scholar? Where is the philosopher of this age? Has not God made foolish the wisdom of this world?" And in 1 Corinthians 1:19 Paul tells us God's attitude toward such people: "I will destroy the wisdom of the wise; the intelligence of the intelligent I will frustrate."

I know there are people who would say, "I got a perfect score on my college entrance exam; therefore, I do not believe in God," or, "I have received a Nobel Prize, so I do not have to believe in God." But consider what Jesus said: "I praise you, Father, Lord of heaven and earth, because you have hidden these things from the wise and learned, and revealed them to little children" (Matt. 11:25). Your brain, on its own, has no power to research God and find him. No, God must enable you to seek him. Additionally, have you ever considered where your brain comes from? Any ability you have, whether it is to think clearly or to reason correctly, is God's common grace to you. It is a gift from God. How, then, can you take your God-given mind and use it to revile, despise, and nullify the Author of all? But the Bible tells us that only those who are humble will receive the truth God reveals to us. Paul said this in 1 Corinthians 2:9–10, "However, as it is written: 'No eye has seen, no ear has heard, no mind has conceived what God has prepared for those who love him'—but God has revealed it to us by his Spirit."

Jesus is the Judge who scatters the arrogant and pulls the mighty ones down from their thrones. He reverses all sinful social order, sending the rich empty away and condemning those who are self-righteous. This righteous Judge came to seek, not the righteous, but sinners. Remember the rich young ruler? He came to Jesus because he wanted to inherit eternal life. The Lord Jesus counseled him to sell his possessions and follow him. This young man refused to submit to the counsel of God and went away sad. Let me tell you, Jesus Christ is good news to the humble, but he is bad news to the arrogant, the mighty, and the rich. To all the latter, he is the righteous Judge.

God Is Merciful

The fourth attribute Mary speaks of is that God is merciful. The word "mercy" appears five times in Luke 1 (vv. 50, 54, 58, 72, 78). Mary reveled in the knowledge of this great attribute of God.

What is grace? It is God's love shown to guilty sinners. But what is mercy? Mercy is God's love shown to guilty sinners who are miserable in their sinful condition. In Exodus 3:7 we read what the LORD—the eternal God, the great I AM THAT I AM—spoke from the burning bush to Moses: "I have indeed seen the misery of my people in Egypt. I have heard them crying out because of their slave drivers, and I am concerned about their suffering." God showed mercy to the Israelites in Egypt and delivered them.

God is merciful to his people today also. So Mary sang, *"His mercy extends to those who fear him"* (v. 50). Let me assure you of one thing: A man will never experience God's mercy if he remains arrogant in the imagination of his heart. But the one who fears God will always receive mercy.

Mary also sang, *"He has helped his servant Israel, remembering to be merciful"* (v. 54). In Luke 1:58, we read that the Lord had shown Elizabeth great mercy. Zechariah also speaks of God's mercy, declaring that God raised up a Savior "to show mercy to our fathers" (v. 72), and celebrating the "tender mercy of our God" (v. 78). Our God is a merciful God.

God Is a Covenant God

The fifth attribute that Mary sings about is that God is a covenant God. We must realize that God did not have to enter into a covenant with sinful man. There is nothing in his being necessitating that he stoop down and promise salvation to anyone. But the truth is, God did just that. He entered into a covenant with Abraham, promising to show mercy to him and his descendants by granting them salvation.

Zechariah spoke of this great promise. Referring to the salvation God was bringing through Christ, he said that God's purpose was "to show mercy to our fathers and to remember his holy covenant, the oath he swore to our father Abraham: to rescue us from the hand of our enemies, and to enable us to serve him without fear in holiness and righteousness before him all our days" (Luke 1:72–75).

Mary referred to God's covenant nature in different words. She said, *"He has helped his servant Israel, remembering to be* merciful," that is, remembering his covenant, *"to Abraham and his descendants forever, even as he said to our fathers"* (Luke 1:54).

In Genesis 12:3, God told Abraham, "All peoples on earth will be blessed through you." This was the covenant God made with Abraham. God was not speaking of Isaac or David, but of Jesus, the Son of Abraham and the Son of David. In a flash, God gave Abraham a revelation of the great salvation that was going to come in the fullness of time in Jesus Christ. Jesus himself said, "Abraham rejoiced at the thought of seeing my day; he saw it and was glad" (John 8:56). Abraham rejoiced at the thought of seeing the fulfillment of the covenant promise God had made to him, and it was fulfilled in the Son God promised to Mary.

God Is Faithful to His Covenant

The sixth attribute Mary speaks of is the faithfulness of God to his covenant. If God makes promises through a covenant, he will fulfill his promises, because he is the God of the covenant.

By the time the virgin Mary was born, two thousand years had passed since God made his promise to Abraham. The kingdom of Judah had ceased to exist six hundred years earlier, and there had been no prophets for four hundred years. All this time passed, yet God's promise remained unfulfilled. The words of the psalmist describe this time as he asks, "Has God forgotten to be merciful? Has he in anger withheld his compassion?" (Ps. 77:9).

Then, suddenly, in the fullness of time, God saw the sin and misery of his people and remembered to be merciful to them. Our God cannot lie; what he promises he will do. Paul writes, "For no matter how many promises God has made, they are 'Yes' in Christ" (1 Cor. 1:20). All of God's promises to us are fulfilled in the indescribable gift of his Son, our Lord Jesus Christ.

Mary realized that what was happening in her womb was the fulfillment of the age-old promise to Abraham to send the divine Messiah, Jesus the Savior, the eternal God incarnate. So she sang, *"He has helped his servant Israel, remembering to be merciful to Abraham and his descendants forever, even as he said to our fathers"* (vv. 54–55).

God Is the Savior

The final attribute Mary describes is that God was her Savior. *"My soul glorifies the Lord and my spirit rejoices . . ."* In what was Mary rejoicing? *"in God my Savior"* (vv. 46–47).

The Bible tells us that all have sinned and fall short of the glory of God. That means Mary herself was a sinner who needed a Savior. Never believe the lie that Mary was not a sinner. She was, and when she discerned what was happening in her womb, she realized that she was going to be the mother of her own Lord and Savior. Jesus Christ, the One who saves sinners—the One who would save his mother, the One who would save Elizabeth, the One who saves all who put their trust in him, whether Jew or Gentile—was in her womb. That is why Mary was filled with what Peter calls "inexpressible joy" (1 Pet. 1:8–9).

Two thousand years after God made his promise to Abraham, the Savior came. Mary knew that it was he alone who could take away sins and destroy the works of the devil. But how would he do these things? By his death on the cross.

At this point we may ask: How can God die? That is a mystery, but that is the whole purpose of the incarnation. God took on human nature in the person of Jesus the son of Mary, and it is in that nature that God can die. We read about this in Hebrews 10:5: "When Christ came into the world, he said, 'Sacrifice and offering you did not desire, but a body you prepared for me.'"

In the fullness of time, the eternal Son took upon himself human flesh in the womb of Mary by the power of the Holy Spirit. Soon he would be born as God/man, and later he would be introduced by John the Baptist as "the Lamb of God who takes away the sin of the world!" (John 1:29). As Paul later wrote, "God made him who had no sin to be sin for us, so that in him we might become the righteousness of God" (2 Cor. 5:21).

This is God's plan of salvation for us. Because God is holy, he must punish sinners. But God is also love, so he does not desire to punish us. But how can God not punish sinners and still be holy? He must punish his own Son, who freely gave himself to be punished for our sins on the cross.

Therefore, Mary said, *"He has brought down rulers from their thrones but has lifted up the humble"* (v. 52). God's Son would reverse all sinful social order, lifting up the humble and putting them on the thrones of the mighty ones. Jesus spoke of this during his earthly ministry, when he preached, "Blessed are the meek, for they will inherit the earth" (Matt. 5:5). In her song, Mary also said, *"He has filled the hungry with good things"* (v. 53). Jesus said later, "Blessed are the poor in spirit," and, "Blessed are those who hunger and thirst for righteousness, for they will be filled" (see Matt. 5).

God reached out with his strong arm in Christ and saved his people from their sins. He did not do that for angels who sinned, but only for the descendants of Abraham. In him, we are forgiven of all our sins and justified forever. In him, we find mercy. In him, we are made children of God. In him, the hungry are filled with his perfect righteousness. In him, we are adopted into God's own family. In him, we enjoy fellowship with God.

That is why Mary was singing, "My *soul magnifies the Lord, and my spirit rejoices in God my Savior."* She was saying that her son, Jesus Christ, would also be her Savior. David said the same thing in Psalm 110:1: "The LORD says to my Lord." Thomas said it in John 20:28: "My Lord and my God!" When we believe in Christ, we will say, "Jesus is my Lord." Without that confession, we cannot be saved.

So Mary sang, "I worship God, I praise God, and I rejoice exceedingly in God, because I know that my Savior is in my womb."

Can You Sing Mary's Song?

What about you? Can you worship and sing this song with Mary? Is Jesus your God? Is Jesus your Lord? Is Jesus your Savior? Or are you arrogant? Do you think you are something because you have a PhD, or because you have political clout, or because you are rich? Let me remind you of one truth recorded in this song: God will pull the mighty down, scatter the arrogant, and send the rich away empty.

If you are not filled with joy unspeakable at the news of the incarnation of Christ, it is because you are coming to him as one who is rich, arrogant, or mighty. He will never help a person who comes to him in that way. God sent his Son to seek and save the unrighteous, miserable, wretched sinners who are conscious of their wretchedness. If you come to him that way, he will fill you with joy unspeakable and full of glory.

Are you fascinated with God's indescribable gift of his Son, Jesus Christ? Are you fascinated by this Mighty One? Can you sing about his attributes and rejoice in them? Do you fear him? Are you hungry for righteousness? Are you poor in spirit? Have you said to him, as Mary did, "I am your humble servant. I submit to you; be it done to me according to your word"?

I urge you to believe on the Lord Jesus Christ and be saved. If you do, you will join the saints of all ages, including Mary, Zechariah, Elizabeth, and Simeon, in singing, "Glory to God in the highest! My soul magnifies the Lord and my spirit leaps for joy in God my Savior. He has shown mercy to me, lifting me up from the ash heap of this world and putting me upon a throne in his kingdom. He sent his Son all the way down to my hell to take me all the way up into his heaven."

If you have not trusted in Christ for salvation, you cannot sing this song. My prayer is that you humble yourself today and come to him, knowing that he is the merciful Savior, the covenant God who is faithful. Yes, he is holy and he is the great Judge, but he is also the Savior, and he will be merciful to those who come to him in repentance and faith. May God help you to believe on the Lord Jesus Christ that you may be saved. Then you also can sing with intelligence and heart concerning God's Son, the indescribable gift sent to us from heaven for our joy, our Lord Jesus Christ.

9
Good News of Great Joy
LUKE 2:1–14

[10]The angel said to them, "Do not be afraid. I bring you good news of great joy that will be for all the people. [11]Today in the town of David a Savior has been born to you; he is Christ the Lord."

Luke 2:10–11

In his book *The God Delusion*, scientist Richard Dawkins says that those who believe in God are deceived. That does not mean Dawkins is not a worshiper. He worships creation rather than the Creator, who is blessed forever (see Rom. 1:25). But the truth is, we are not the deluded ones. The Bible speaks about the deceitfulness of sin. Not only that, the Bible also says that the people of this world who are without God also are without hope. Dr. Dawkins can preach only bad news and pessimism. A mere material universe cannot give us good news.

Today I bring you good news of great joy—news of our heavenly Father's gift to us. This gift is his own Son. This gift is wrapped in flesh, wrapped in rags, wrapped in grave clothes, and finally, wrapped in eternal glory. During the Christmas season, many will unwrap gifts given by parents, friends, and relatives. Some gifts may disappoint; others will give joy for a season.

The gift that heaven gives us also needs unwrapping. In the eighth century BC, Isaiah prophesied, "For to us a child is born, to us a son is given . . . the Prince of peace" (Isa. 9:6).

Our need is not for material things. We are in need of a divine person, one described by John Murray as "the conjunction . . . of all that belongs to Godhead and all that belongs to manhood," who was "'in the likeness of sinful flesh' (Rom. 8:3)." Murray says this one was "made of the seed of David according to the flesh" (Rom. 1:3), "made of a woman" (Gal. 4:4), "made in the likeness of men" (Phil. 2:7), "manifested in the flesh" (1 Tim. 3:16)." Murray concludes, "[Christ] came into the closest relation to sinful humanity that it was possible for him to come without thereby becoming himself sinful."[15] As the apostle John declares, "The Word became flesh and made his dwelling among us" (John 1:14).

This divine person was the firstborn child of the virgin Mary. The virgin birth is a distinctive Christian doctrine. And when we unwrap this gift, we will experience great, everlasting joy. This unwrapping calls for the assistance of the Holy Spirit and the full resources of our mind, will, and affections. Luke the historian received this glorious truth of the virgin's Son from the virgin Mary herself while he was in Judea researching for his gospel.

We want to speak about three things: the good news promised, the good news performed, and the good news proclaimed.

The Good News Promised (Luke 1:26-38)

The angel Gabriel was sent to a poor yet pious girl in her early teens who lived in Nazareth of Galilee. The angel told Mary that she had found grace in the sight of God—grace that caused her to rejoice and be addressed as "blessed." He said that she would be pregnant and give birth to a son, though she was a virgin. Mary then asked how a virgin could conceive without knowing a man. Gabriel told her that God the Holy Spirit would accomplish it.

God explains what is puzzling to man. Are you baffled by the miracles of creation, the virgin birth, the resurrection, the new heaven and new earth? The answer to all these puzzles is God. God created all things, God caused the virgin to conceive, God raised Jesus Christ from the dead, God will raise us also up from the dead, and God will create a new heaven and a new earth.

---

15 John Murray, *Collected Writings*, vol. 2, *Systematic Theology* (Edinburgh: Banner of Truth, 1977), 133.

"Nothing is impossible with God," Gabriel told Mary, harking back to the Lord's own words to Sarah: "Is there anything too hard for the LORD?" (Gen. 18:14). This is God's explanation for all the miracles recorded in the Scriptures.

Unlike the aged Zechariah, the teenager Mary believed God's word of promise, saying, "I am the Lord's servant. May it be to me as you have said" (Luke 1:38). She confessed what every believer must confess, that the triune God is Lord and we are his slaves. We are to surrender to God and do his will alone. In fact, Paul called himself "*Paulos doulos Christou Iēsou*," "Paul, a slave of Christ Jesus." Have you confessed with your mouth, "Jesus is Lord, and I am his slave"? Have you said with Mary, "Thy will be done in me"?

The son of Mary is the Son of God to whom is given the throne of David. He is the everlasting King. This Son will conquer all evil and usher in the kingdom of peace for all his people. In the Son, God is visiting his people to save them from all their enemies. This Son is the gift of God, the seed of the woman, who came to crush the head of the dragon. He is the seed of Abraham in whom all the families of the earth will be blessed. He is the seed of David. He is Jesus, the son of Mary.

God chose this name for him. Through Eve, a woman who was deceived, a curse came into the world. Through Mary, a woman who believed, a Son came into the world, bringing eternal blessings to all his people. He was, as John Murray says, the product of a supernatural begetting; he was a supernatural person; and he was supernaturally preserved from all defilement.[16]

Mary trusted God's word in spite of what this virginal conception and birth could bring to her, including shame, slander, alienation, poverty, divorce, and even death by stoning. She trusted God to deal with any problems that would come about due to her faith in the promise of God.

Do you trust God in spite of the cross and trials it will assuredly bring? Jesus said, "In this world you will have trouble. But take heart! I have overcome the world" (John 16:33).

---

16 John Murray, *Collected Writings*, vol. 2, *Systematic Theology* (Edinburgh: Banner of Truth, 1977), 134–135.

The Good News Performed (Luke 2:1–7)

Centuries before, Micah had prophesied the exact location of the birth of the Messiah: "But you, Bethlehem Ephrathah, though you are small among the clans of Judah, out of you will come for me one who will be ruler over Israel, whose origins are from of old, from ancient times" (Mic. 5:2). In the fullness of time, the eternal Son was to be born in Bethlehem because the Son of David must be born in the city of David. The supernatural person took upon himself perfect human nature. As Jesus declared, "Before Abraham was born, I am!" (John 8:58). He is the "I AM WHO I AM" in human flesh (see Exod. 3:14).

It was God's decree that the Messiah be born in Bethlehem. But how could a poor, pregnant girl from Nazareth, betrothed to a very poor son of David, give birth to Jesus in Bethlehem, eighty miles south of Nazareth? God himself brought it to pass.

Caesar Augustus was emperor of Rome from 27 BC to 14 AD. He was born Gaius Octavian, the grandnephew of Julius Caesar, who adopted him as his son. He later became the first emperor of Rome and was the architect of Pax Romana, having put an end to all civil wars. In 27 BC the senate gave him the title Augustus, "Exalted One," which may also mean "Divine." Called savior and lord by the people, Augustus was the most powerful person in the world at that time. Of his own free will, he sent out a decree that a census for taxation purposes should be taken in all the Roman Empire. In Judea, every person was required to go to the birthplace of his forefathers.

This decree of Caesar Augustus brought Joseph and Mary to Bethlehem, the city of David, for registration. This happened so that Jesus the Messiah could be born there in fulfillment of God's word through Micah. Caesar Augustus, the emperor of the Roman Empire, gave a decree to fulfill the decree of God the Father, the Sovereign of the universe. The same was true of Judas, the Pharisees, the scribes, the Sanhedrin, the high priests, and Pilate when they handed over Jesus Christ to be crucified for our salvation.

Caesar Augustus gave the external peace of Pax Romana. Yet the philosopher Epictetus said, "While the emperor may give peace from war on land and sea, he is unable to give . . . peace of heart, for which man yearns more than even for outward peace."[17] God sent his Son in the fullness of time to give us this peace of heart.

Joseph and Mary arrived early in Bethlehem. Soon after they arrived, she began to experience contractions and the time came for her to give birth. They urgently began knocking on the doors of various homes in Bethlehem, looking for a room and privacy for the birth of this child. But no one wanted this couple to upset their ordered lives. Who wants to hear the cry of a newborn baby? Who wants to have an unclean woman in the house? Who wants to serve as a midwife to help and comfort the mother? The Bethlehemites behaved like the priest and the Levite, who passed on the other side when they saw the injured traveler left for dead on the road (Luke 10). They had no room for Mary and her son. They did not want to get involved. John later spoke of this: "He came to that which was his own, but his own did not receive him" (John 1:11).

This poor couple had a home in Nazareth. But in Bethlehem they were homeless. Many years later Jesus would say, "Foxes have holes and birds of the air have nests, but the Son of Man has no place to lay his head" (Luke 9:58). Yet, finally, he too found a place to lay his head—on the cross. Paul tells us, "For you know the grace of our Lord Jesus Christ, that though he was rich, yet for your sakes he became poor, so that you through his poverty might become rich" (2 Cor. 8:9).

Finally, Jesus was born in a cave where the cattle were kept. Mother Mary herself wrapped him in rags and laid him in a manger. There lay God in the feeding trough. He became homeless that we might have a home in God, as later he promised: "Do not let your hearts be troubled . . . . In my Father's house are many rooms; if it were not so, I would have told you. I am going there to prepare a place for you" (John 14:1–2).

The Good News Proclaimed (Luke 2:8–20)

The most important event in the history of the world was the birth of the Son of God. Heaven itself announced this birth. Just as we send out birth announcements to friends and relatives, so

17   Norval Geldenhuys, *Commentary on the Gospel of Luke*, New International Commentary on the New Testament series (Grand Rapids: Eerdmans, 1979), 112.

God also announced the birth of his Son, Jesus, the son of David and the son of Mary. To whom did he disclose this marvelous event? Not to Caesar Augustus or Herod the king or the Sanhedrin or even the high priest. The first shall become last and the last first. God chose to disclose this stupendous salvific event to the despised shepherds of Bethlehem, who were caring for the sheep to be sacrificed in the temple.

Orthodox Jews looked upon shepherds as being ceremonially unclean. They were seen as liars and were forbidden from giving witness in court. Yet God chose the lowly shepherds to hear the gospel from the angels. In 1 Corinthians 1, we find the way God deals with human beings:

> Brothers, think of what you were when you were called. Not many of you were wise by human standards; not many were influential; not many were of noble birth. But God chose the foolish things of the world to shame the wise; God chose the weak things of the world to shame the strong. He chose the lowly things of this world and the despised things—and the things that are not—to nullify the things that are, so that no one may boast before him. It is because of him that you are in Christ Jesus, who has become for us wisdom from God—that is, our righteousness, holiness and redemption. Therefore, as it is written: "Let him who boasts boast in the Lord." . . . Where is the wise man? Where is the scholar? Where is the philosopher of this age? Has not God made foolish the wisdom of the world? (1 Cor. 1:26–31; 20)

Through the angels, God unwrapped the gift of his Son to these nothings, the despised shepherds. So also he unwraps this gift to us, who are also nothings. I believe the interpreting angel was Gabriel, who had also spoken to Mary.

Who Is this Gift?

Who is this baby wrapped in rags and lying in the feeding trough in a cave?

- *He is the Holy One* (Luke 1:35). Unlike us, Jesus was born sinless, by supernatural preservation, and he lived a sinless life so that he could save sinners.

- *He is the Son of God* (Luke 1:32, 35). The pre-existent, eternal Son in his incarnation made himself poor by taking upon himself human nature. Isaiah calls him "Mighty God, Everlasting Father, Immanuel, God with us" (see Isa. 9:6, 7:14). Micah says he is the one "whose origins are from of old, from ancient times" (Mic. 5:2). He is the great I Am.

- *He is the Christ* (Luke 2:11), the Messiah, the Anointed Deliverer promised in the Old Testament, who defeats all our enemies and sets the captives free. He binds the strong man to set us free and proclaims the year of jubilee that will have no end.

- *He is Lord* (Luke 2:11). He alone is God and Sovereign. The one lying in a manger, wrapped in rags, is Yahweh, the God of Israel. As John Murray said, the Creator of all became creature and the immortal became mortal. God was put to sleep in the animals' feeding trough.

- *He is the everlasting King* (Luke 1:32–33), in fulfillment of the Davidic covenant. God promised David that one of his sons would become the eternal King. Isaiah says, "Of the increase of his government and peace there shall be no end" (Isa. 9:7). Jesus rules forever over all. No one can be saved without fully embracing his absolute kingship. "Surrender to him and be saved," is the message of Gabriel.

- *He is the Savior* (Luke 2:11). The Old Testament spoke of God as Savior. Mary praised him as "my Savior" (Luke 1:47). Mary was a sinner who needed a savior, and Mary's son would save her from all her sins. Caesar was also called a savior, but he was impotent to save people from their sins. This baby wrapped in rags and sleeping in heavenly peace was sent to save sinners. There is no other savior.

- *He is Jesus* (Luke 1:31). His name, which means "the Lord saves," was chosen, not by Mary or Joseph, but by God the Father himself. He is the greater Joshua, whose mission is to save his people from their sins (Matt. 1:21).

Have You Opened this Gift?

Are you one of his people? Then he will save you. God became man that he may die for our sins. He was crucified because the wages of sin is death. Jesus Christ, God/man, died in our place so that we sinners, enemies of God, might be reconciled to God and enjoy peace with God, peace with others, and peace within. Paul says, "God made him who had no sin to be sin for us, so that in him we might become the righteousness of God" (2 Cor. 5:21).

Micah prophesied concerning this Messiah who would be born in Bethlehem, "And he will be their peace" (Mic. 5:5).

Jesus Christ is our peace. He achieved this peace for us through the cross, as Paul explains:

> For he himself is our peace, who has made the two one and has destroyed the barrier, the dividing wall of hostility, by abolishing in his flesh the law with its commandments and regulations. His purpose was to create in himself one new man out of the two, thus making peace, and in this one body to reconcile both of them to God through the cross, by which he put to death their hostility. He came and preached peace to you who were far away and peace to those who were near. For through him we both have access to the Father by one Spirit. (Eph. 2:14–18)

This peaceful, sleeping baby, wrapped in rags, would soon be wrapped in grave clothes. He had to die that we may die in peace. But he would also leave his grave clothes to be wrapped in glory. All of heaven, therefore, sang with great joy in the presence of God the Father: "*Glory to God in the highest, and on earth peace among those of God's good pleasure*" (Luke 2:14).

In time, this baby would reveal the glory of God as none had ever done before. Jesus prayed to his Father, "I have brought you glory on earth by completing the work you gave me to do" (John 17:4). It is he who taught us to pray, "Our Father who art in heaven, hallowed be thy name." The purpose of God, Isaiah said, would be fulfilled in this Messiah.

"*Peace on earth among those of God's good pleasure*" means salvation through Christ comes to the elect of God by divine initiative through his Son, the only Savior. The great fear due to our sin against God is replaced by great joy which shall be to all people—all who make room for Jesus in their hearts through repentance and faith, all who respond to this gospel as Mary and the despised shepherds did.

May God help us all to unwrap this gift package from heaven, which came to us in the fullness of time. It is the divine Person, the Holy One, the Son of God, Christ the Lord, the Eternal King, our Savior. His name is Jesus, the hope of this world. He is no longer wrapped in rags or grave clothes, but in glory, and is seated on the right hand of God. Soon he shall come again in glory to this earth to save his people and judge his enemies. Therefore, I plead with you to make room for him. He will take your miserable, confused, peaceless, disorganized life and set you right. Receive him today in your heart, that you may join Mary and Joseph and the angels and the shepherds in glorifying and praising God with eternal praise. In Luke 7, Jesus told the sinful woman, "Your sins are forgiven; go in peace." He says the same to us: "Your sins are forgiven; go in peace." May we all go in peace today as we celebrate Christmas.

10
Receive the Greatest Gift

LUKE 2:8–14

[13]Suddenly a great company of the heavenly host appeared with the angel, praising God and saying, [14]"Glory to God in the highest, and on earth peace to men on whom his favor rests."

Luke 2:13–14

During election times, some American politicians express their love for Jesus in order to seduce the evangelical electorate into voting for them. One candidate declared that he considered Jesus as his philosopher, and that statement no doubt gave him the vast majority of the evangelical vote. But we do not read in the Bible that Jesus was known as a philosopher. Philosophers are commonplace. Imagine what would have happened to this man had he confessed, "Jesus Christ is my Savior and Lord. I obey, worship, and serve him."

The gospel of Luke tells us in the first two chapters about the person of Jesus Christ and his birth. Throughout the world, Christmas is celebrated as a time of great joy, with people getting together to eat and drink and give presents to each other. Most people have no clear idea of the significance of this season. It is just another holiday to celebrate. But Christmas points to the greatest event in history: the incarnation of Jesus Christ.

History cannot be understood without the biblical revelation of creation, fall, and redemption. God triune, who existed from all eternity, alone is self-existing, self-sufficient, infinite, personal Being. God created the worlds and all that is in them, including human beings, and permitted sin to enter the world. When

Adam and Eve sinned, all creation fell and became subject to God's wrath.

But God also has a plan of redemption for man and the cosmos. This redemption is accomplished through a man, Jesus Christ, the second Person of the holy Trinity. Because of sin, man must die, for "the wages of sin is death" (Rom. 6:23). It is not negotiable. Only a man can redeem sinful men by dying their death. But such a redeemer must also be sinless and infinite in order to redeem all elect sinners of the world. Our redeemer, therefore, must be God/man.

The Old Testament promised such a man would redeem us by defeating and destroying the devil, the enemy of all good. In the *proto-euangelion* of Genesis 3:15, we read that the seed of the woman will crush the head of the serpent. Genesis 22:18 tells us this man will be the seed of Abraham in whom all the families of the earth will be blessed. Second Samuel 7 tells us he is the Son of David, an everlasting King. Isaiah tells us he will be the son of a virgin (Isa. 7:14) and a son given by God (Isa. 9:6), upon whose shoulders will be the government of the world. Luke 1:34 reveals to us that this seed of the woman is the son of virgin Mary. John tells us, "In the beginning was the Word, and the Word was with God, and the Word was God. . . . The Word became flesh and made his dwelling among us. We have seen his glory, the glory of the One and Only, who came from the Father, full of grace and truth" (John 1:1, 14).

In his Son, God sent the greatest gift for sinners like us. So Paul exclaims, "Thanks be to God for his indescribable gift!" (2 Cor. 9:15). The greatest event in all human history is the coming of a Savior from heaven to earth. Without his coming, there is no meaning to history. Jesus came into the world to save the world from divine destruction.

The Place and Time

The virgin Mary gave birth to Jesus in Bethlehem in a cave where cattle were kept. What is the significance of the incarnation of God's Son? Professor John Murray defined the incarnation as follows:

The incarnation means that he who never began to be in his specific identity as Son of God, began to be what he eternally was not. . . . The infinite became the finite, the eternal and supratemporal entered time and became subject to its conditions, the immutable became the mutable, the invisible became the visible, the Creator became the created, the sustainer of all became dependent, the Almighty infirm. . . . [In sum], God became man.

[The incarnation] is the conjunction in one person of all that belongs to Godhead and all that belongs to manhood.[18]

J. Oliver Buswell, Jr. says, "The virgin birth was a special miracle wrought by the Third Person of the Trinity, whereby the Second Person of Trinity, the eternal Son of God, took to himself a genuine and complete human nature, and was born as a man, without surrendering in any way his complete divine nature."[19] Anyone who denies the incarnation is an antichrist (1 John 4:2–3).

The Son did not come to indwell a human being as the Holy Spirit does, nor did he take the place of a human soul. The Son took to himself a human soul and body. The Son became the man Christ Jesus and his manhood is permanent. Because he was sinless, he obeyed God actively and passively, vicariously and representatively. Hence, Paul could say for our eternal comfort and joy, "Christ died for our sins and was raised for our justification" (Rom. 4:25).

The virgin Mary delivered the baby in the Bethlehem cave in Joseph's presence during the reign of Caesar Augustus in Rome. Augustus was the grandnephew of Julius Caesar, who adopted him so that he became heir to the throne. Known as Augustus Julius Caesar Octavius, he ruled for fifty-seven years (43 BC–AD 14) and was the sole ruler of the Roman Empire from 27 BC to AD 14. Jesus was born around 7 BC, before the death of Herod the Great in 4 BC.

It was a time of Roman peace, the Pax Romana, established by Rome's conquest of all her enemies. Caesar Augustus was

18 John Murray, *Collected Writings of John Murray*, Vol. 2, Select Lectures in Systematic Theology (Edinburgh: Banner of Truth Trust, 1977), 132–133.

19 J. Oliver Buswell Jr., "The Virgin Birth of Christ" in *Baker's Dictionary of Theology*, edited by Everett F. Harrison et al (Grand Rapids: Baker, 1982), 543–544.

called savior, and many recognized him as a divine son of god, "imperator of land and sea, the benefactor and savior of the whole world"[20] Caesar Augustus gave an order that all the world should be registered for purposes of taxation and military service. Thus, Mary and Joseph traveled to Bethlehem from Galilee to register.

But Caesar Augustus was under the Sovereign God of the Bible. All these events occurred because it was the Sovereign God's will that the Savior should be born in Bethlehem, the city of David, as was revealed in Micah 5:2 seven hundred years before Caesar Augustus' order went out. All this happened to redeem a fallen world: "But when the time had fully come, God sent his Son, born of a woman, born under law, to redeem those under law, that we might receive the full rights of sons" (Gal. 4:4–5).

The Celebrants

In Luke 2, we see that God himself celebrated the birth of Jesus. The news of Christ's birth was not sent to Herod the Great, the Sanhedrin, or Emperor Caesar Augustus. None of them was invited to celebrate the first Christmas. Ignoring the centers of power, God invited some poor shepherds of Bethlehem who were watching their sheep by night. Shepherds belonged to the bottom of society. Like publicans, they were the pariahs and untouchables of the day. They were unclean because they could not keep the ceremonial laws. Because they were seen as thieves and liars, they were forbidden to give witness in a court. Yet God invited these who were considered great sinners to hear the gospel and celebrate the birthday of his Son.

This is always the way of God. God gave the greatest honor of becoming the mother of our Lord to a thirteen-year-old virgin who came from a poor, undistinguished family. Mary herself spoke of this: "My soul glorifies the Lord and my spirit rejoices in God my Savior, for he has been mindful of the humble state of his servant. From now on all generations will call me blessed" (Luke 1:46–48). So also he chose the most undeserving shepherds to hear the gospel and celebrate and proclaim the birth of Jesus.

---

20 Joel B. Green, *The Gospel of Luke*, New International Commentary on the New Testament (Grand Rapids: Eerdmans, 1997), 125.

Our God feeds the hungry, but he sends the rich away empty; he lifts up the humble and puts down the arrogant; he gives grace to the humble and opposes the proud; he justifies the ungodly and condemns the self-righteous.

We read about this way of God throughout the Scriptures. James says, "Listen, my dear brothers: Has not God chosen those who are poor in the eyes of the world to be rich in faith and to inherit the kingdom he promised those who love him?" (James 2:5). Paul tells the same story: "Brothers, think of what you were when you were called. Not many of you were wise by human standards; not many were influential; not many were of noble birth. But God chose the foolish things of the world to shame the wise; God chose the weak things of the world to shame the strong. He chose the lowly things of this world and the despised things—and the things that are not—to nullify the things that are, so that no one may boast before him" (1 Cor. 1:26–29). If we have not submitted to Jesus Christ, it is because we are rich and arrogant. But God sends the rich empty away and puts down the proud. He rejects the mighty.

The mighty of Bethlehem rejected this Savior. John writes, "He came to that which was his own, but his own did not receive him" (John 1:11). The mighty reject him, and he rejects the mighty. If we have not bowed down to Christ, then we are including ourselves among the mighty, self-righteous, arrogant, and rich. We are rejecting the gift of God's Son. We are exchanging the knowledge of the gospel for that which is evil and a lie.

There was no room for the Son of David among the mighty in Bethlehem, so the angel came by night to the lowly shepherds who were outside with their flocks. When we read the gospel account carefully, we see that God himself, with his entourage of a multitude of angels, came to the celebration: *The glory of the Lord shone around them*" (Luke 2:9). There was the annunciation of the Lord to the poor, wretched, unclean shepherds. When God speaks to sinners, whether through an angel or directly, we are filled with great fear. We read this of Zechariah, of Mary, and, now, of the shepherds. Why this great fear? Because God is holy. Isaiah confessed when he saw God's glory, "I am undone. I am sinful. I must die" (see Isa. 6:5). How can a sinner stand in the glory of God's presence?

The Remedy for Fear

These shepherds were terrified with *"great fear"* (Gk., Luke 2:9). How can we be delivered from our great fear of eternal death? The only remedy is hearing and believing the gospel. The angel said, *"Today I bring you good news of great joy. . . . Today in the town of David a Savior has been born to you; he is Christ the Lord"* (Luke 2:10). The happiest person on earth is a Christian. He alone has reason to rejoice with great joy.

We need to hear the gracious gospel, which the shepherds heard first: "Fear not! You will not die eternally. You will not go to hell and experience God's wrath. Someone else will die and go to hell in your place. This One who is born will suffer and die in your place as your representative. He is your mediator, atonement, and high priest. So do not be afraid; I bring you, for your benefit, good news of great joy."

Instead of great fear, there was now great joy among the shepherds. We also must hear and believe this good news so that we may experience everlasting joy. Through the divine Son, the wrath of God has been removed from us. Our fear, our death, and our hell are gone.

Who Is This Baby?

This good news of great joy is about an infant born in Bethlehem. He is the Son of God wrapped in flesh and in strips of used clothing, lying in a cattle-feeding trough. Who is this baby? Certainly, he is not a mere philosopher. We are all philosophers, in a sense, but the philosophy of most is the philosophy of the fool who says in his heart, "There is no God" (Ps. 14:1). But this One is no mere philosopher. Yes, he is a human being who entered history, but he is much more. The angel revealed to Mary that her son was to be named Jesus (Luke 1:31), which means "Jehovah is salvation." The fulfillment of God's promise has come in Jesus, the One who saves God's people from their sins. This baby is Jesus, the only Savior of the whole world.

Moreover, it was revealed to Mary that this One is the Son of the Most High, which means he is the second Person of the Trinity, God himself in human flesh. This is not the description of a mere philosopher. Away with all such notions of Jesus Christ! He is God himself.

Additionally, Gabriel declared to Mary that this child is the eternal King of the house of David, in fulfillment of God's covenant with David (2 Sam. 7:16) and the Isaianic prophecies (Isa. 6, 7, 9, 11). He is the eternal King who conquers all his enemies and rules his people beneficently. His people will submit to him, be subject to him, confess him, serve him, and sing his glorious praise. He will not tolerate any enmity in his kingdom, and his kingdom has no end.

Mary was also told that this one is the Holy One. Jesus was sinless; thus, he alone was fit to be our Savior and atonement. Paul writes, "God made him who had no sin to be sin for us, so that in him we might become the righteousness of God" (2 Cor. 5:21).

The angel also revealed to the shepherds that this homeless infant wrapped in used clothing and lying in a cattle trough in a cave is the Savior. Caesar Augustus could not save anyone or give them peace. He could proclaim himself savior, but that did not make it so. Jesus alone can give peace and joy as no one else can. Do not call him philosopher; he is the only true Savior.

Why do we need a Savior? Because we are fallen, guilty sinners, under God's wrath, and we must die unless someone else takes the guilt of our sins and dies our eternal death. All have sinned, including the virgin Mary, thus we all need a Savior. The shepherds of Bethlehem represent all elect sinners. To them, God announced that he had sent a Savior—his greatest gift to mankind. In him, we receive grace and salvation.

We need grace. The angel greeted Mary, "Rejoice, you who are filled with grace" (Luke 1:28, author's translation). Mary is not the source of grace, but she received grace to the full. Why should Mary rejoice? Because she was filled with grace and found grace with God. We see the same expression used of Noah, Zechariah, and the shepherds: they found grace with God. We need grace, for salvation is by grace.

In Luke 1:30 we read, "Do not be afraid, Mary, you have found grace with God." The antidote to our great fear is receiving the gospel of God's everlasting grace. The Old Testament promised a Savior. Isaiah pictures Yahweh as Savior of his people. This Yahweh we now see is Jesus. Salvation is found in no one else in the whole universe. Jesus is the only Savior of the world, of all who will repent and believe. There is no other savior. Everyone must trust in this Savior to be saved.

This is good news of great joy, good news that gives great joy, not just for some, but for all the people. No wonder the Samaritans confessed that Jesus is the Savior of the world (John 4:42). In the seed of Abraham, Jesus Christ, all the families of the earth are blessed. John writes, "God so loved the world that he gave his one and only Son, that whoever believes in him shall not perish but have eternal life" (John 3:16).

"Today in the town of David a Savior has been born to you; he is Christ the Lord" (Luke 2:11). Today! No longer do we need to look for the fulfillment of God's promise of a Savior. Christ has come. He is born today. We have a Savior in whom every promise is fulfilled. Today is the day of fulfillment, the day of celebration, the day of salvation, the day of great joy. We are blessed because we live today, and that today will continue until Jesus comes again. Paul writes, "Now is the time of God's favor, now is the day of salvation" (2 Cor. 6:2). To Zacchaeus, Jesus said, "Today salvation has come to this house" (Luke 19:9). And to the thief who confessed him on the cross, Jesus declared, "Today you will be with me in paradise" (Luke 23:43). Let us praise God for today! Today is your day of salvation. But your today will end when you die. I beseech you in the name of Jesus to receive him and be saved today.

This infant wrapped in flesh and used clothes, lying in a trough, is none other than Christ, the promised Messiah. He is the Anointed One, equipped and qualified to be the Prophet, Priest, and conquering King. John says Jesus was filled with the Holy Spirit without measure (John 3:34). He is the promised deliverer who delivers us from our guilt, misery, death, and slavery. He himself said in Luke 4:18, citing Isaiah 61, "The Spirit of the Lord is on me, because he has anointed me to preach good news to the poor. He has sent me to proclaim freedom for the prisoners and recovery of sight for the blind, to release the oppressed, to proclaim the year of the Lord's favor."

Are you poor? Then the good news is preached for you. Are you a prisoner? He will set you free. Are you blind? He will give you sight. Are you oppressed by the devil? He will release you from your oppression and set you free, and if the Son sets you free, you are free indeed. It is he who proclaims the year of the Lord's favor, that is, the year of the Lord's grace. Rejoice greatly, you poor, you prisoners, you oppressed, you blind, you deaf, you dead. Do not be afraid. Rejoice!

This helpless, dependent, poor infant is also Lord. That means he is God, Yahweh. He is Creator God, Redeemer God, and covenant Lord. He is all-sovereign; all things are put under his feet.

Good News! The Lord Has Come!

What, then, was the message of the angel? The Lord has come! The King has come! The Savior has come! The Messiah has come! Let us bow down before him, surrender to him, and serve him. This is good news of great joy! Isaiah predicted this several times:

> You who bring good tidings to Zion, go up on a high mountain. You who bring tidings to Jerusalem, lift up your voice with a shout, lift it up, do not be afraid; say to the towns of Judah, "Here is your God!" See, the Sovereign LORD comes with power, and his arm rules for him. See, his reward is with him, and his recompense accompanies him. He tends his flock like a shepherd: He gathers the lambs in his arms and carries them close to his heart; he gently leads those that have young. (Isa. 40:9–11)

> How beautiful on the mountains are the feet of those who bring good news, who proclaim peace, who bring good tidings, who proclaim salvation, who say to Zion, "Your God reigns!" Listen! Your watchmen lift up their voices; together they shout for joy. When the LORD returns to Zion, they will see it with their own eyes. Burst into songs of joy together, you ruins of Jerusalem, for the LORD has comforted his people, he has redeemed Jerusalem. The LORD will lay bare his holy arm in the sight of all nations, and all the ends of the earth will see the salvation of our God. (Isa. 52:7–10)

> After the suffering of his soul, he will see the light of life and be satisfied; by his knowledge my righteous servant will justify many, and he will bear their iniquities. (Isa. 53:11)

This One would bring glory to God in the highest. That is what the angels were singing. He would honor God the Father with complete trust and obedience, and God's purpose would prosper in his hand. He would do all things for God's glory, including dying on the cross to fulfill God's purpose of saving sinners justly. Jesus prayed to the Father, "I have brought you glory on earth by completing the work you gave me to do" (John 17:4). No other human being could so glorify God, but Christ did. Glory to God in the highest!

Adam and all his fallen descendants dishonored God, but Jesus came to glorify God, and he accomplished that purpose. So the angels sang, *"Glory to God in the highest,"* meaning this infant would bring glory to God. He also would, finally, bring peace on earth by establishing peace between God and sinners. God and sinners were reconciled by the cross on which Jesus died. Jeremiah calls him, "The LORD Our Righteousness" (Jer. 23:6), and Micah says of this ruler born in Bethlehem, "He will be their peace" (Mic. 5:5). Not only does he bring about peace between God and man, but he also brings peace between man and man. So now a husband and wife can live together in love, without divorce. We can have a community of believers who will love one another and lay down their lives for one another. It is all because of this infant who would die on the cross for the sins of the world.

The angel brought this good news to the shepherds. Now we, and all true ministers, preach the same good news, which Jesus and his apostles preached: "Behold, your Savior, Christ the Lord." The Bible says salvation is of the Lord; salvation is of the Jews. Salvation comes to us by Jesus the Jew, who was crucified, has risen, and is reigning.

How Should We Respond?

What should be our response to this good news? We should believe it as Mary believed. When the angel came to her, she responded, "I am the Lord's slave. . . . May it be to me as you have said" (Luke 1:38). Mary trusted God for everything. What about the shepherds? They believed. Luke 2:15–20 describes how they hurried to Bethlehem, searched for the baby, found him, and published the message: "This baby is our Savior, our Christ, our

Lord, who destroys all our fears and grants us great joy. He is the great liberator." They surrendered to this Jesus and worshiped him.

Mary was a sinner who trusted in her Son, the Savior. Elizabeth also trusted in this infant while he was still in Mary's womb. When Mary came to her, she said, "Blessed are you among women, and blessed is the child you will bear! But why am I so favored, that the mother of my Lord should come to me?" (Luke 1:42–43). She confessed the infant in the womb of Mary to be her Lord.

What should be our response to grace? Believe and receive the Savior. In Romans 10, Paul speaks about the necessity of a preacher called by God to preach the gospel, because faith comes by hearing the gospel, and we must believe the gospel to be saved. We must confess with our mouths, "Jesus is Lord," and believe in our hearts that God raised him from the dead, and we will be saved (Rom. 10:9). We must call upon the name of the Lord.

There are only two responses to the gospel message when it comes to us: We can either receive it, or we can reject it. We will either surrender, believe, worship, and receive him as Lord and Savior, or we will continue in our rebellion, unbelief, and enmity.

I urge you not to see Jesus as a philosopher; rather, confess him as Savior, Christ the Lord. And be aware that this Jesus is also the Judge. He has come into the world as "the stone cut not by human hands" whose purpose is to destroy all powers of the world that oppose God's kingdom (see Dan. 2).

This stone will fall on all rebels who oppose God. Therefore, stop your rebellion now. Fall down and kiss the Son. Believe in him, and receive the grace of God. If you surrender, you will be saved. If you resist, you will be destroyed. Who can stand the wrath of the Lamb? The answer is, no one. I plead with you to receive God's indescribable gift, our Lord Jesus Christ, who, though rich, for our sakes became poor so that we, through his poverty, might become rich.

I received this gift long ago, but I am still unwrapping it. Jesus makes me happy every day. Do not give me stuff, but tell me about Jesus, the Savior, Christ the Lord. It is my prayer that he will also be your Savior, your Christ, your Lord today.

11
The Christmas Story
LUKE 2:8–20

The shepherds returned, glorifying and praising God for all the things they had heard and seen, which were just as they had been told.

Luke 2:20

Luke 1 spoke about the miraculous virginal conception of the peace-child. This miracle brought about, in due time, the virgin birth of Jesus Christ, the King of the world. Luke writes about this birth in Luke 2. We want to examine several points from this passage.

The Time and Place of Christ's Birth

Jesus was born during the reign of Caesar Augustus, the Roman emperor. It was predicted by the prophet Micah that Jesus was to be born in Bethlehem (Mic. 5:2). In God's sovereignty, Augustus issued a decree (Gk., *dogma*) that a census be taken of the whole Roman Empire to facilitate the full collection of taxes. In obedience to this dogma, Joseph traveled with the pregnant Mary from Nazareth of Galilee to Bethlehem, where Jesus was born.

Caesar Augustus, the emperor, was in fact serving the newborn King of kings by ordering the census. Born as Gaius Octavian, Augustus was the grandnephew and later adopted son and designated heir of Julius Caesar. Ruling as emperor from 27 BC to 14 AD, he was acclaimed as the architect of Pax Romana. The famous Myrian inscription speaks of him in this manner: "Divine Augustus Caesar, son of a god, imperator of land and sea, the benefactor and savior of the world."[21] In other words, Augustus was acclaimed as god, savior, and king.

But Jesus Christ, the infant born in Bethlehem, is infinitely superior to Augustus. He is the true God and Savior, not a pretended one. He is the eternal Lord and King. He was the born King of the world and is the King of kings and Lord of lords. His dominion alone is universal and eternal.

Jesus Was Born in a Stable

Christ was born, not in a mansion in Rome or Jerusalem, but in a place where cattle were kept. As an adult, he said, "The Son of Man has no place to lay his head" (Matt. 8:20). Here at his birth there also was no place for him in the inn or in a private home to lay down his infant head.

Luke emphasizes the manger by referring to it three times. Jesus was probably born in a cave or a cow shed in Bethlehem, the city of his ancestor David. When he was born, Mary wrapped him in strips of worn-out clothes to keep his limbs straight. Ezekiel speaks of the common infant care, which was not given to the nation of Israel: "On the day you were born your cord was not cut, nor were you washed with water to make you clean, nor were you rubbed with salt or wrapped in cloths" (Ezek. 16:4). But Mary did all these things for the infant Jesus.

Thus, the King of kings, the eternal God, was laid, not in a golden cradle, but in a feeding trough for animals. His parents were very poor, which we conclude from Luke 2:24, because they could only offer a sacrifice of a pair of doves (see Lev. 12:8).

A tradition going back to the second century located the birth of Jesus in a cave in Bethlehem. Emperor Constantine erected a basilica in Bethlehem over a likely cave, which has been excavated under the present Church of the Nativity.

The Great Birthday Celebration

There was a great celebration at Jesus' birth, beginning with an announcement, followed by great singing. This celebration

---

21 Joel B. Green, *The Gospel of Luke*, New International Commentary on the New Testament (Grand Rapids: Eerdmans, 1997), 125.

took place not in the daytime in Jerusalem in the temple, but in a field in Bethlehem at night. No kings, princes, priests, scribes, Pharisees, nobles, wise, or mighty were invited. Instead, God invited the nothings of the world: in this case, some wretched, despised, unclean, poor shepherds.

These shepherds were considered to be unreliable witnesses, thus they were not permitted to give testimony in court. Yet God chose them to be witnesses of Christ's birth. They were considered unclean because they could not keep themselves ceremonially clean as they worked with the sheep. Yet these shepherds, as well as publicans and prostitutes, were invited to enter into Christ's kingdom, which is "righteousness, peace and joy in the Holy Spirit" (Rom. 14:17).

All sinners who acknowledge they are sinners are invited to Christ's birthday celebration. The angel of the Lord, therefore, appeared to these shepherds who were keeping their flocks. These sheep were destined for temple sacrifices. But the birth of Jesus would put an end to all such animal sacrifices.

I believe the angel of the Lord in this account was Gabriel. So there was Gabriel and there were the poor, despised shepherds with their animals. God the Father himself was there, for we are told, *"The glory of the Lord shone around them"* (v. 9). This was nothing less than the shekinah glory of God appearing for the birthday celebration of his Son, Jesus Christ.

The angel proclaimed the gospel to the poor sinners, who were deeply afraid. How many people live in deep fear due to their sins! Adam and Eve were afraid because of their guilt. But the gospel drives out all our sin-caused fears. So the angel said, *"Stop being afraid, because I proclaim to you good news, the gospel of great joy, which shall be to all people, that is, all people of the world"* (v. 10, author's paraphrase). The gospel of great joy is the antidote to the great fear caused by our great sin against our great God.

What is the good news? *"Today is born to you a Savior, Christ the Lord, in the city of David"* (v. 11). Isaiah prophesied about this: "For to us a child is born, to us a son is given" (Isa. 9:6). He is given for us, for our benefit. So the angel was declaring, "Today is born *to you*." Luke uses the dative of advantage, meaning "for your benefit," "for your salvation." Christ was born for our benefit and for the benefit of the whole world. Jesus is called Savior only twice in all the gospels: here in Luke 2:11, and in John 4:42, where he is called the Savior of the world.

Then the angel gave two signs to increase the shepherds' faith. First, he said, they would see this Savior, Christ the Lord, *"wrapped in cloths and lying in a manger"* (v. 12). This Jesus was the only newborn infant who was lying in a manger in the city of David, probably surrounded by animals.

Second, they saw and heard the choir of heaven singing. After speaking to the shepherds, the angel Gabriel joined an army of angels to sing in worship of this God who was sending his Son to earth to reconcile sinners to himself through his atonement. The angels were singing to celebrate the birth of God's Son. But they also sing continually, daily, at the rebirth of sinners. Jesus declared, "In the same way, I tell you, there is rejoicing in the presence of the angels of God over one sinner who repents" (Luke 15:10). I pray that because of your repentance, heaven will rejoice and the angels will sing even this day. Whenever a sinner comes to know Jesus as Savior and Lord, there is great singing, celebration, and joy in heaven in the presence of the angels and of God our heavenly Father.

The angels' song spoke of the result of Christ's birth: *"Glory to God in the highest, and on earth peace for men of God's favor"* (v. 14). God's glory was revealed when he sent his eternal Son as an infant to make atonement for the sin of the whole world. Therein lies the glory of God. Jesus would live for God's glory, fulfilling all God's law, and he would die for God's glory. So he would declare, "I have brought you glory on earth by completing the work you gave me to do" (John 17:4). When he died on the cross, he said, *"Tetelestai*—It is finished!" The work of God—the work of redemption—was finished.

I pray we will not forget God the Father, who did not spare his own Son for our salvation. Let us join the celestial beings to give God the glory that is due his name. The angels sang, *"On earth peace for all of God's chosen ones."* Such people will be given grace to repent and believe in Jesus Christ, the Savior of sinners. If a person is not saved, it is because he refuses to acknowledge that he is a sinner. God will never save a person who will not confess that he is a sinner.

But thank God, he does save sinners. And such people will enjoy God's three-dimensional peace. First, they experience peace with God. Their war with God is over. All enmity ceased when Jesus dealt with our sins on Calvary's cross. No longer enemies, we are now friends, yea, children of God. Second, we experience peace with the people of God, especially with those in the church, with whom we are united in the bond of peace. Third, we now have peace within ourselves. True shalom comes to us through Christ's life and death. Because of our Father's action, we can enjoy this peace now and for all eternity. So "peace" is speaking about all the blessings associated with the coming of Jesus Christ into this world.

What Is the Gospel?

What is the gospel, the good news of great joy sung about by the angels? It has to do with a person, God's incarnate Son. We think there are many things we have to know, but there is only one thing needful. Do you know the gospel? Do you know Jesus Christ and what he has done? This newborn alone can solve our terrible sin problem.

What is the gospel? Paul says, "[Christ] was delivered over to death for our sins and was raised to life for our justification" (Rom. 4:25). He also writes, "For what I received I passed on to you as of first importance: that Christ died for our sins according to the Scriptures, that he was buried, that he was raised on the third day according to the Scriptures" (1 Cor. 15:3–4). Isaiah declared, "You who bring good tidings to Zion, go up on a high mountain. You who bring good tidings to Jerusalem, lift up your voice with a shout. Lift it up! Do not be afraid! Say to the towns of Judah, 'Here is your God!' . . . How beautiful on the mountains are the feet of those who bring good news, who proclaim peace, who bring good tidings, who proclaim salvation, who say to Zion, 'Your God reigns!'" (Isa. 40:9; 52:7).

Our God reigns for us! Therefore, burst into songs of joy! Isaiah says, "The Spirit of the Sovereign LORD is on me, because the LORD has anointed me to preach good news to the poor. He has sent me to bind up the brokenhearted, to proclaim freedom for the captives and release from darkness for the prisoners, to proclaim the year of the LORD's favor" (Isa. 61:1–2). And in Isaiah 9:4–6 he speaks about the great joy that is going to come to Zion, for the people of God, because of three reasons. First, God is going to break our yoke and bars (Isa. 9:4). Jesus himself said, "Come unto me, all those who are weary and heavy laden, and I will give you rest" (Matt. 11:28). He has broken our yoke of slavery to sin and Satan. Second, the war is over (Isa. 9:5). The equipment of war is being burned up because Christ fought the war and won. Third: "For to us a child is born, to us a son is given" (Isa. 9:6). This Son will finish his job of redemption.

Our God comes to fight and win. He comes in Jesus, preaching good news to the poor. The gospel reveals the person and work of Christ, who set us free from all shackles and burdens.

The Names of Christ

Who is this child born, this son given to us? He has many names because it is impossible to comprehend the nature of the eternal Son of God. But let us look at some so that we can know better who he is. The more we know him, the more we can rejoice with unending joy.

HE IS IMMANUEL ("GOD WITH US")

John writes, "The Word became flesh and dwelt among us" (John 1:14). He is very God and very man; he is not a God so transcendent that he does not want to come to us. He came to us in Jesus Christ. He is God down here with us, God who comes to help us in all our troubles. Paul says, "But if Christ is in you . . ." (Rom. 8:10). So he is Immanuel, God with us, God about us, and more than that, God who has taken up residence in us.

HE IS SAVIOR

This child is Savior, not only of the poor shepherds but of all the elect sinners of the world. This Savior accomplishes our salvation and applies it to us. God himself was called Savior in the Old Testament (Isa. 45:15, 21). Only God can save us from our sins, and he does so. Jesus Christ is God and Savior. This infant is God who saves.

HE IS JESUS

Interestingly, Gabriel did not tell the shepherds the name Jesus. This was the name given by God his Father to Joseph: "You are to give him the name Jesus, because he will save his people from their sins" (Matt. 1:21). In him, all the families of the earth will be blessed (Gen. 12:3). He saves us from all our sins so we can stand before God without sin and clothed in his divine righteousness. If we have trusted in Christ, we can now stand before God, in exceeding joy, without shame or fear.

HIS NAME IS CHRIST

This infant is the Spirit-anointed promised deliverer. As the Holy Spirit came upon him, he was anointed and qualified to be the anointed Prophet, giving us the true revelation of God. He is truth and speaks truth, and we find this truth when we open the Bible. We believe in the authority of the Bible. He is also the anointed Priest, our great high priest, a priest without sin. And not only is he the perfect priest, but he is also the perfect victim. It was Christ's sacrifice that reconciled us to God. He is our propitiation and intercessor. Even now he prays for us in the heavenly places. He is also the anointed King. Being the adopted firstborn of Joseph, he is the legal heir to David's throne. His kingship is forever. He has universal dominion. Micah foretold his kingship: "But you, O Bethlehem Ephrathah, though you are small among the clans of Judah, out of you will come for me one who will be ruler over Israel, whose origins are from of old" (Mic. 5:2). He is the eternal God become man.

HE IS THE LORD (YAHWEH)

In the Old Testament, the Hebrew name *Yahweh* is translated in the Septuagint by the Greek word *Kurios*, which is later applied to Jesus. When we say, "Jesus is Lord," we mean, "Jesus is God." The infant Jesus that we see lying in a feeding trough in Bethlehem is God himself.

HE IS CALLED WONDERFUL COUNSELOR

That means he is divine, supernatural Counselor (Isa. 9:6). He is God the Counselor. The Spirit of counsel will rest upon him (Isa. 11:2). He is a wonderful strategist whose plan defeats all strategies of his enemies. His plan for our salvation was successful, including his death on the cross, because he rose again, having conquered all his enemies. What a wonderful Counselor! Paul declares, "Oh, the depth of the riches of the wisdom and knowledge of God! How unsearchable his judgments, and his paths beyond tracing out! 'Who has known the mind of the Lord? Or who has been his counselor?' 'Who has ever given to God, that God should repay him?' For from him and through him and to him are all things. To him be the glory forever! Amen" (Rom. 11:33–36).

He Is Mighty God

This One is the warrior God (Isa. 9:6). Woe unto us if he opposes us, for he will always win! As the seed of the woman Mary, he crushed the head of the serpent, defeating the prince of this world and destroying the one who holds the power of death. He came to destroy the devil, our slave-master. He did, and freed us from slavery to sin and Satan. We read, "The LORD is a warrior; the LORD is his name. Pharaoh's chariots and his army he has hurled into the sea. The best of Pharaoh's officers are drowned in the Red Sea" (Exod. 15:3–4). Paul writes, "Having disarmed the powers and authorities, he made a public spectacle of them, triumphing over them by the cross" (Col. 2:15). This child is God Almighty, the champion fighter. So go ahead, challenge him! Call him out! He will fight you, and you will lose. Surrender is our only option. Yet losing and surrendering is also our salvation. May we therefore bow down to him and confess him as Lord. The psalmist exhorts, "Kiss the Son, lest he be angry, and you be destroyed in your way, for his wrath can flare up in a moment. Blessed are all who take refuge in him" (Ps. 2:12).

He Is the Everlasting Father

According to the customs of the Near East, every king was seen as the royal father of the nation. The title "Everlasting Father" (Isa. 9:6) reveals that Christ's paternal care for his royal subjects never ends. It is eternal. So we read, "But you are our Father, though Abraham does not know us or Israel acknowledge us; you, O LORD, are our Father, our Redeemer from of old is your name" (Isa. 63:16). The psalmist tells us, "As a father has compassion on his children, so the LORD has compassion on those who fear him" (Ps. 103:13). He cares for his children with a father-like compassion. He never stops loving us, though his love includes divine discipline for our good.

HE IS THE PRINCE OF PEACE

This child is the prince who defeats all his enemies through war and ushers in everlasting peace (Isa. 9:6). It is not a win-win situation. Christ always wins, and sinners always lose. Micah says he is our peace (Mic. 5:5). This peace was achieved for us by his death on the cross. So Paul writes, "God was pleased to have all his fullness dwell in him, and through him to reconcile to himself all things, whether things on earth or things in heaven, by making peace through his blood, shed on the cross" (Col. 1:19–20). Peace comes at a high cost, and Jesus paid the highest price for our peace. Isaiah concludes by saying, "Of his government and peace there will be no end" (Isa. 9:7). His government will increase to fill the whole cosmos. That is why, if we do not surrender to him and embrace his government now, we will have no peace now or at the moment of our death. True peace comes to us only through surrender to the Prince of peace.

HE IS THE SHEPHERD

Micah tells us, "He will stand and shepherd his flock in the strength of the LORD. . . . And they will dwell securely" (Mic. 5:4). He is the shepherd who will care for his flock, as we read in Ezekiel 34. There we are promised that God will shepherd us himself, and he does so through Jesus Christ. Jesus said, "I am the good shepherd," and then he says he will do what no other shepherd has ever done in the history of the world: "The good shepherd lays down his life for the sheep" (John 10:11). He will be with us as we walk through the valley of the shadow of death and will bring us to dwell with God forever. Those who never believed in Jesus Christ will walk through the valley of death, but believers will walk through the valley of only the *shadow* of death. That is why we must ask you: Do you believe this gospel the angel proclaimed and sang in God's glorious presence, in the hearing of the poor shepherds—the gospel regarding Jesus and his saving work?

The Faith of the Shepherds

The shepherds believed what the Lord declared through the angelic host. Leaving their sheep in God's care, they hastened to Bethlehem in search of Jesus. The Lord promises, "You will find me when you seek me with all your heart" (Jer. 29:13). These shepherds sought Christ with all their heart, and they found him, lying in a manger. Then they preached the gospel to Mary and Joseph and others, telling them what the angels had said: *"Born today in Bethlehem in a manger is a Savior for us, Christ the Lord."*

What was the reaction of King Herod to the news of the baby's birth? He was troubled (Matt. 2:3), and along with him, all Jerusalem was troubled. In fact, Herod wanted to kill Jesus. That is the attitude of many people today, though no one can kill God. Others were amazed at the news. Yet mere amazement is not faith.

But Mary treasured and pondered the gospel in her heart. She meditated on it to discover the full meaning, and she discovered it. This son in the manger would be her Savior, her Christ, and her Lord. Salvation had come to the house of Joseph, as it would later come to the house of the publican Zacchaeus (Luke 19).

The shepherds believed and returned to their fields, glorifying and praising God. To all who believe, the gospel gives great joy in the Holy Spirit. They praised God for honoring them in this way. These lowly shepherds were nothing in the eyes of the world, yet God's favor rested on them. They were chosen from the foundation of the world, and on them God lavished his grace.

What can we do for such gospel salvation? Grace to us brings praise to God, a praise that is unceasing. That is the reason we worship God.

Conclusion

We must understand who Jesus is. Do not feel sorry for this infant lying in the manger. Later on, he himself would say, "Do not weep for me; weep for yourselves and for your children" (Luke 23:28). Friends, we either believe the gospel, or we do not. We either surrender to this mighty God, or we do not. We either treasure and ponder the gospel, or we do not. And we will either rejoice exceedingly, or live in the gloom of divine wrath, depending on whether we honor God's Son by repentance and faith, or dishonor him through unbelief.

Let us be like the shepherds. Let us believe the gospel and praise God for his great salvation. Let us say, "Come, Lord Jesus. Live in me as Lord and Savior forever." Let us join with the songwriter: "You ask me how I know he lives; he lives within my heart."

May we therefore come as empty vessels and ask the Lord to fill us with himself and with his grace. May we live for his glory from this day forward. A child has been born to us, a son has been given to us to bless us, and we are truly blessed.

12
Who Is This Child?

JOHN 1:1–18

¹In the beginning was the Word, and the Word was with God, and the Word was God. ²He was with God in the beginning. ³Through him all things were made; without him nothing was made that has been made. ⁴In him was life, and that life was the light of men. . . . ¹⁴The Word became flesh and made his dwelling among us. We have seen his glory, the glory of the One and Only, who came from the Father, full of grace and truth.

John 1:1–4, 14

Did you know God wants us to seek him? He says so throughout the Bible. For example, in Amos 5 we read, "Seek me and live. . . . Seek the LORD and live. . . . Seek good, not evil, that you may live" (Amos 5:4, 6, 14). But how can mortal man seek God? How can sinners go to heaven and appear before the majesty of God? They cannot do so on their own. God had to send his Son to seek us so that we, in turn, may seek him and live.

As we study John's gospel, I pray that God will open the eyes of unbelievers that they may behold the glory of God in the face of Jesus Christ. And I pray that God will grant those whose eyes he has already opened greater perception so that they may know more of God, experience greater joy and peace in God, worship God with greater reverence, and obey God with ever-increasing zeal.

The Most Important Question

Who is Jesus Christ? In the fullness of time, about two thousand years ago, a baby was born of a woman, born under the law. We are told in Luke 2 that this baby, Jesus Christ, was wrapped in rags and placed in a manger in Bethlehem, the city of David.

Who is Jesus Christ? This is the question we must ask today, and it is the question Jesus himself asked his disciples in Caesarea Philippi: "Who do people say the Son of Man is?" They replied, "Some say John the Baptist; others say Elijah; and still others, Jeremiah or one of the prophets." Then Jesus asked his disciples, "But what about you? Who do you say that I am?" and Peter, representing the disciples, replied, "You are the Christ, the Son of the living God" (Matt. 16:13–16).

The question "Who is Jesus Christ?" is the most important question in the world. Why? Because our eternal destiny depends upon how we answer this question. In John 1:1–18, which is the prologue to the gospel of John, the apostle John gives a very clear description of who Jesus is.

John's gospel is addressed to unbelievers and is written for the purpose of revealing the person and work of Jesus Christ to them so that they may trust in him and receive eternal life. We find this stated in John 20:30–31, "Jesus did many other miraculous signs in the presence of his disciples, which are not recorded in this book. But these things are written that you may believe that Jesus is the Christ, the Son of God, and that by believing you may have life in his name."

As we study John's description of Christ in John 1:1–18, we must acknowledge that John was not giving us his opinion. Rather, under the inspiration of the Holy Spirit, John was speaking from God as he was being carried along by the Holy Spirit (2 Pet. 1:21). John's gospel, like all Scripture, "is God-breathed and profitable for teaching, rebuking, correcting and training in righteousness" (2 Tim. 3:16).

Therefore, whenever we think about Jesus, and especially when we celebrate the Christmas season, we must ask, "Who is this baby wrapped in rags and placed in a manger? Who is this one who, when he was a grown man, said, 'The Son of Man has no place to lay his head'"? Let me assure you, not everyone will give the same answer. The vast majority of people, when they think of Jesus, will curse him, reject his claim, and come under judgment. But others, a minority, will fall down before him in humility, faith, repentance and worship, and will exclaim, "My

Lord and my God!" It is my prayer that you will belong to the latter category of people.

Jesus Is Eternal

Who is Jesus Christ? In John 1:1 we read, *"In the beginning was the Word"* (Gk., *"en archē ēn ho logos"*). What is meant by the phrase *"in the beginning"*? It points not to the beginning of creation but to timeless eternity. *"In the beginning"* speaks about the preexistence of Christ. It means he was before the creation, before the universe was made. He is eternal.

Jesus spoke about his eternal existence when he prayed, "And now, Father, glorify me in your presence with the glory I had with you before the world began" (John 17:5). And in John 17:24 Jesus said, "Father, I want those you have given me to be with me where I am, and to see my glory, the glory you have given me because you loved me before the creation of the world." This helpless baby is from eternity. There was no time when he was not.

Jesus is not only eternal, but he is the eternal Word. He is the One about whom John said, *"In the beginning was the Word."* What is the purpose of words? The purpose is to express the speaker's thoughts and reveal those thoughts to others. So we can understand from John's statement that Jesus is the one who reveals God to us. Without him, we cannot truly know God.

Jesus Christ is the Word of God personalized. In Psalm 33:6 we read, "By the word of the LORD were the heavens made," and in Revelation 19:13 we read, "He is dressed in a robe dipped in blood, and his name is the Word of God." This Word reveals God's thoughts to us.

When John says, *"In the beginning was the Word,"* he is telling us that Jesus Christ, the Word, the Revealer of God to us, is eternal. The created world is not eternal, but Jesus Christ is. He is the Cause and Creator of everything in the universe.

Jesus Was with God

Next, John tells us, *"The Word was with God"* (v. 1). In the Greek text we read, *"ho logos ēn pros ton theon"* ("the Word was *toward* God").

This statement tells us that Jesus Christ is equal to God the Father, but also distinct from him in terms of personality. God exists as one God in three Persons: God the Father, God the Holy Spirit, and Jesus Christ, the Word. This is a difficult concept for human beings to understand, but it is what God's infallible word declares.

Additionally, when John says, *"The Word was with God,"* he implies that a certain intimacy, fellowship, and communion exists between Christ, the Holy Spirit, and God the Father. Jesus spoke about this intimacy when he prayed, "And now, Father, glorify me in your presence with the glory I had with you before the world began" (John 17:5). In verse 18 we read, *"No one has ever seen God, but God the One and Only, who is at the Father's side, has made him known."* Physical creatures cannot see the invisible being of God. Not even Moses saw God. But this verse tells us that the Son of God enjoyed communion with God the Father from all eternity and has revealed him to us.

The Persons of the Godhead are equal and yet distinct in terms of personality. Jesus said, "When the Counselor comes, whom I will send to you from the Father, the Spirit of truth who goes out from the Father, he will testify about me" (John 15:26). Here we see the Trinity: God the Father; Jesus Christ, the Word, the One and Only, the only-begotten Son; and the Holy Spirit, who proceeds from the Father and the Son.

Jesus Is God

John continues, *"and the Word was God."* (v. 1). In the Greek, it is *"theos ēn ho logos."* The predicate nominative, *theos,* is placed first, which means the emphasis is on the subject, *"ho logos,"* ("the Word"). Without the article (*ho*), it would say "God is the Word," but here God is the predicate.

This phrase also speaks about the plurality of persons in the unity of God's being—he is one God in three distinct Persons. There is great intimacy, fellowship, and communion within the Godhead in these three Persons. Some people say, "God is love, and so he had to create human beings so that he could love them and be loved by them." But God did not need to create anything. Within the three Persons of the Godhead there is full, satisfying love and fellowship.

What have we learned so far about Jesus Christ, the Word? We know that the Word is God and has always existed as God. We know that the Word is uncreated Deity. Do you still want to curse him, blaspheme him, disobey him, and treat him with contempt? I caution you: This Word is God, in whom all the fullness of Deity dwells. He is the uncreated, self-existing, self-sufficient, infinite, eternal, personal God. I hope you will not mock him or attempt to philosophize him away.

Jesus Is Life

John continues, "*Through him all things were made*" (v. 3). John is telling us that the Word created everything visible and invisible. This speaks against the philosophies of monism, pantheism, and the eternality of matter. The world had a beginning given to it by the Word. It also tells us Jesus is not a part of creation; rather, he is the Creator through whom all things were made.

In verse 4, John writes, "*en autō zōē ēn,*" meaning "*in him was life.*" This Word is the source of all life. Do you want life? It is to be found in him. He embodies all life, both physical and spiritual.

Who, again, is this Word? We read his name in verse 17: Jesus Christ. This baby is the source of all life. We breathe because of him. "*In him was life.*" Jesus spoke of this many times. In John 14:6, he said, "I am the way and the truth and the life." In John 10:10, he revealed the purpose of his coming into this miserable, wretched world of darkness and death and destruction: "The thief [the devil] comes only to steal and kill and destroy; I have come that they may have life, and have it to the full."

No wonder Jesus declared at the tomb of Lazarus, "I am the resurrection and the life" (John 11:25). When he commanded, "Lazarus, come out!" the dead man came forth. Why? Jesus Christ is life, and he gives life.

Jesus Is Light

The next thing John writes is "*kai hē zōē ēn to phōs tōn anthrō-pōn,*" meaning "*and that life was the light of men*" (v. 4). The Word is the light who gives us general revelation and special revelation of God. Jesus Christ gives us general revelation through creation, through which we can know his everlasting power and divinity. But he also gives us special revelation of God the Father through his life and death. This knowledge comes to us only through the Revealer, the Word, Jesus Christ.

John tells us, *"The true light that gives light to every man was coming into the world"* (v. 9). The Word, the second Person of the Trinity, is the true revelation of God to us. He is the ultimate light. He is not the moon; he is the Sun, the very source of light (see Mal. 4:2; Rev. 21:23). And we are told that he "shines." The verb is in the present tense in the Greek. Jesus is shining right now, even in the midst of the darkness of moral corruption, falsehood, errors, cults, religions, and philosophical speculations of the world. The light of Christ is now shining for you and for me.

Verse 9 also teaches us that none of us will be able to give God an excuse for not receiving his Son, for the true light *"gives light to every man."* The Word has given revelation of God to us through creation as well as through the declaration of the gospel, which centers on his life and his death. Jesus is the light that enlightens every person. Without the Word, there would not be any light in our fallen world. The Word has come into the world to enlighten all people, and all people are responsible for this knowledge. As human beings, we are responsible for how we respond to Jesus Christ. Either we worship him, adore him, fall down before him, and believe in him, or we curse him and are eternally damned. It is this same Christ to whom all judgment is given.

In Hebrews 1, we also read about this ultimate, perfect, final revelation of God that has come to us in Christ:

> In the past God spoke to our forefathers through the prophets at many times and in various ways, but in these last days he has spoken to us by his Son, whom he appointed heir of all things, and through whom he made the universe. The Son is the radiance of God's glory and the exact representation of his being, sustaining all things by his powerful word. After he had provided purification for sins, he sat down at the right hand of the Majesty in heaven. (Heb. 1:1–3)

Jesus is the only true light who can give light, the revelation of God, to all men. In John 1:18 we read, *"No one has ever seen God."* God is spirit, and a physical human being cannot see him. Yet one person has seen him: "*God the One and Only*," Jesus Christ. He is God, "*who is at the Father's side.*" The phrasing speaks about the intimacy and fellowship that Christ enjoys with his Father. He alone knows the Father comprehensively, and so it is he alone who can exegete, that is, explain or interpret, God the Father to us. Only through Christ can we understand that God loves sinners, as we read in John 3:16: "God so loved the world that he gave his one and only Son, that whoever believes in him shall not perish but have everlasting life." He is the exegete par excellence, the only one who is able to reveal God the Father to us. This revelation is not comprehensive, but it is sufficient for our salvation.

Jesus is the interpreter of God the Father to us, and so we must also understand that the words and deeds of Christ recorded in the Scriptures are really the words and deeds of God the Father. Jesus said, "Anyone who has seen me has seen the Father" (John 14:9). Knowing the Son is knowing the Father.

The Word Became Flesh

In verse 14 we read, "*kai ho logos sarx egeneto*," meaning "*the Word became flesh.*" We have seen that this Word was from all eternity; now we learn that, in time, the Word became flesh. Without abandoning or compromising his deity, God the Son took upon himself human nature in body and soul. The incarnation of Christ is essential to the Christian faith. In 1 John 4:2–3, John tells us that anyone who denies that Jesus has come in the flesh is a heretic, an antichrist.

Why did the divine second Person of the Trinity take upon himself frail human flesh? So that, as our representative, he might fully obey God and procure salvation for all who believe in him. Just as the first Adam disobeyed God, and in this Adam all have sinned and come short of the glory of God, now Jesus, the last Adam, came as our representative to fully obey God so that all who believe in him can be saved. Christ became flesh that he might be the mediator between God and man. He who is God had to become a man so that he could die for our sins.

How did the Word become flesh? It was not through the agency of man. This Word became flesh through the mighty operation of the Spirit upon Mary of Nazareth. In Luke 1 we read,

The angel said to her, "Do not be afraid, Mary, you have found favor with God. You will be with child and give birth to a son, and you are to give him the name Jesus. He will be great and will be called the Son of the Most High. The Lord God will give him the throne of his father David, and he will reign over the house of Jacob forever; his kingdom will never end." "How will this be," Mary asked the angel, "since I am a virgin?" The angel answered, "The Holy Spirit will come upon you, and the power of the Most High will overshadow you. So the holy one to be born will be called the Son of God." (Luke 1:30–35)

The incarnation of Christ is a supernatural work of God. It is not man becoming God, but rather God becoming man.

Though he had a human nature, Jesus was without sin. In John 8:46, Jesus asked the Jews, "Can any of you prove me guilty of sin?" In John 8:29, he said he always pleased the Father. Again, in John 15:10 Jesus said, "If you obey my commands, you will remain in my love, just as I have obeyed my Father's commands and remain in his love." He was tempted, but he did not yield to Satan. God became flesh, John says, and *"made his dwelling among us"* for thirty-three years.

We Beheld His Glory

What else does John say about this Word, the Lord Jesus Christ? *"We beheld his glory"* (v. 14). No one beholds Christ's glory unless his eyes are opened by God himself. God opened the eyes of the apostles so that they could see the glory of God in the face of Jesus Christ.

In John 2, we read how Jesus turned water into wine by his mighty power. In verse 11 we read, "This, the first of his miraculous signs, Jesus performed in Cana in Galilee. He thus revealed his glory, and his disciples put their faith in him." Throughout his gospel John describes signs performed by Jesus that reveal his glory.

In John 11:4, Jesus spoke about the sickness of his friend Lazarus: "When he heard this, Jesus said, 'This sickness will not end in death. No, it is for God's glory so that God's Son may be glorified through it.'" He knew he was going to perform a miracle that would help people to understand that he was more than a mere man. In John 11:40, Jesus told his disciples, "Did I not tell you that if you believed, you would see the glory of God?" Then they witnessed the great miracle of Lazarus coming out of the tomb.

So when John wrote, "*We beheld his glory*," he was speaking as an eyewitness of the glory of Christ shown in his teachings and miracles. "Who is this man?" the disciples asked as they saw him walk on water, calm a storm, heal the sick, and raise the dead. What was their conclusion? Jesus is God.

Full of Grace and Truth

In verse 14 John also tells us that the Word was "*full of grace and truth.*" Grace is God's mercy to undeserving, miserable, wretched sinners who merit hell and damnation. God offers us grace through the person and work of Jesus. Because Christ died for our sins and was raised for our justification, we can now receive God's grace.

Do you need God's grace, salvation, hope, peace and life? I do. But how do we obtain them? They come to us only through Christ. We already read that life is to be found only in him, and here we read that grace and truth are also found in him.

Jesus offered this grace to the Jews, but they refused to accept it. Relying on their own righteousness, they said, "No, we prefer Moses because Moses was the one who gave us the law, and, as descendants of Abraham, our responsibility is to keep the law. We have no need for Jesus Christ and the kind of grace you are speaking about—grace for undeserving people. Aren't we the ones who are keeping God's law? If so, then we are quite deserving and have full confidence that God will recognize and reward our righteousness. Who needs grace?"

Oh, how blind such people are! Sinful man can never be saved by his own works of righteousness. John writes, "*For the law was given through Moses; grace and truth came through Jesus Christ*" (v. 17). Can the law impart life, hope, and joy to miserable sinners? No. The purpose of the law, which is holy, just, and good, is to make us conscious of our sin and total depravity. It was never intended to save anyone, and it cannot do so.

God did not stop with giving us the law. He also sent his Son, in whom is life and the fullness of grace and truth. Jesus alone is life; he is the One who can make us alive.

In John 10:10, Jesus said, "The thief comes only to steal and kill and destroy," and, "I have come that they may have life." Yes, there is darkness, death, and misery in the world, but in Christ there is also good news of great joy to all people everywhere. God so loved the world that he sent his Son, and in him is life, grace and truth. A great plenitude of grace and truth can be found in Jesus Christ.

What was the purpose of the incarnation of Christ? Christ became man to make us righteous through his obedience and to grant us forgiveness through his death. It was also designed to give us grace, to give us light, and to open our eyes so that we understand truth.

John says, *"In him was life, and that life was the light of men"* (v. 4). All other religions are false; all human philosophies are nothing. They pretend to enlighten and save us, but they can never introduce us to the one and only God who alone can save us.

Who Is Jesus?

John tells us that this child is life and light, grace and truth, the eternal, perfect God and man. But if you asked Jesus himself, "Who are you and why did you come?" what would he say?

Jesus said he is the *"I AM."* He told the Jews, "If you do not believe that I am, you will indeed die in your sins" (John 8:24). In the Greek, Jesus said, *"Egō eimi,"* which is found in the Septuagint in Exodus 3:14 when God told Moses, "I AM WHO I AM." *"Egō eimi"* means "I am," but its deeper meaning is "I AM, meaning I am the same God who appeared to Moses in the bush. I am the self-sufficient, self-existing, eternal God." When Jesus said, "I AM," he was telling the Jews that if they did not believe that he was God appearing in the flesh, they would not be saved.

This is what "I AM" means, and this is how the Jews of Jesus' time understood that expression. In John 8:58, Jesus used the same words when he declared, "I tell you the truth, before Abraham was born, I am!" Did the Jews think Jesus was calling himself God? Yes. That is why they immediately picked up stones to stone him for the sin of blasphemy.

There are other answers that Jesus gave to the question of who he is:

- "I am the bread of life" (John 6:35). Jesus is the bread who gives us spiritual life.

- "I am the light of the world" (John 8:12). Jesus said he is the light who enlightens us; there is no other.

- "I am the gate" (John 10:9). Jesus is the only way to God. He is the gate, the door, that gives us access to God the Father. No one can go to the Father without going through Jesus Christ.

- "I am the good shepherd" (John 10:14). It is Jesus who feeds us, guides us, and protects us.

- "I am the resurrection and the life" (John 11:25). This baby is the resurrection and the life. Not only does he raise those who are spiritually dead and give them life, but he also raises those who are physically dead from the grave.

- "I am the way" (John 14:6). Jesus said, "I am the way and the truth and the life. No one comes to the Father except through me." Only through Christ can we have fellowship with God.

- "I am the true vine" (John 15:1). Jesus was saying, "I am the one who nurtures you." Every branch is nurtured by the vine; in this case, Jesus is the vine and we are the branches.

Recognizing Jesus

In summary, John's gospel tells us that Jesus is the eternal God, the Creator of all things. He is life and light, the eternal Son, and the second Person of the Trinity. He is the Son of God, the Messiah, the Anointed One, and the King of Israel, as Nathanael declared (John 1:49). He is the Son of Man spoken of in Daniel who came to the Ancient of Days and was given all authority, kingdom, and worship (Dan. 7:13–14). He is the Savior of the world, as the Samaritans confessed in John 4:42, and the Holy One who is without sin, as we read in John 6:69.

What should we do when we recognize who Jesus is? In John 9, we read about Jesus healing a man who was born blind. When the formerly blind man saw Jesus, he did something that I hope you will do also when God opens your eyes to see the glory of God in the face of Jesus Christ. In verse 38, we read, "Then the man said, 'Lord, I believe,' and he worshiped him." This man was born blind, and Jesus gave him physical sight. But Jesus also gave him spiritual sight, and the man's response was to say, "Lord, I believe," and worship Christ. That is the proper response when we recognize who Jesus is. Did Jesus tell the man, "Don't worship me, because I am just an angel" or "I am just a man"? No. He accepted the man's worship because he knew he is God and worthy of all worship and praise.

In John 20, we find doubting Thomas. His eyes were opened to recognize who Jesus was. In verse 28, we read, "Thomas said to him, 'My Lord and my God!'" That is the proper confession we must make. Then we must worship him. That is beholding the glory of God in the face of Jesus Christ.

Who Do You Say Christ Is?

In John 12:47, Jesus said he came to save, not condemn, the world. In John 10:10, he said he came to give life. We must remember that Satan always kills and destroys, but Jesus saves and gives life.

In John 1:11, John says this baby, this Word of God, *"came to that which was his own,"* meaning his own world and especially his own people, *"but his own did not receive him."* The vast majority of people are interested only in trivializing and mocking Christianity. Jesus came to his own world, the world he created and maintains, and to his own people. Yet we are told that they rejected him. They called him a Samaritan, a demon-possessed man, a crazy person, a blasphemer, a lowly carpenter, and a glutton. But by the revelation God gave him Peter said, "You are the Christ, the Son of the living God" (Matt. 16:16). John, in essence, was saying the same thing when he declared, *"We have seen his glory, the glory of the One and Only, who came from the Father, full of grace and truth"* (v. 14). The wretched, sinful Samaritan woman confessed that Jesus was the Christ (John 4). The blind man who was healed by Jesus said, "Lord, I believe," and worshiped him (John 9:38). Thomas, a person full of doubt, was given enough proof that he exclaimed, "My Lord and my God!" and worshiped him (John 20:28).

If you do not want to have anything to do with Jesus Christ, I urge you to consider what he said in John 5:28: "Do not be amazed at this, for a time is coming and now has come when the dead will hear the voice of the Son of God and those who hear will live" (author's paraphrase). The Lord Jesus Christ is going to come with a shout, with the voice of an archangel, and with the sound of the trumpet, and all who are in their graves will hear his voice and come out. Everyone will come out on that day: all philosophers, politicians, and the rich and poor people of the world. All who loved Jesus will come out, and all who mocked Jesus will also come out. Those who have done evil will rise to be condemned, while those who have done good will rise to live (see also 1 Thess. 4:16–17).

What is the one thing needful in this life? We must be born again: *"born not of the will of man, not of the will of flesh, not of the will of a husband, but born of God"* (v. 13). If you are born again, it means God has performed a miracle and your eyes have been opened. Only then will you look at Christ, fall down before him, and confess, "Lord, I believe!"

We began by asking the question, "Who is Jesus Christ?" We have learned that he alone is the eternal One, the Revealer of God, God himself, the Bringer of light and life, grace and truth. He is the Word who became flesh and dwelt among us, whose glory we beheld. How will you respond to this truth? My prayer is that you will believe on the Lord Jesus Christ today and be saved.

13
Jesus Christ, God Incarnate
John 1:1–18

In the beginning was the Word, and the Word was with God, and the Word was God. . . . The Word became flesh and made his dwelling among us.

John 1:1, 14

Who can describe God? Rabbi Ben-Sira asked this question centuries ago, but could not supply an answer. Philosopher Plato also thought about it, telling his students that perhaps someday a word, a *logos*, would come forth from God who would reveal all mysteries and make everything plain.

In due time, the Bible disclosed the identity of the One who would reveal all things: He is the Lord Jesus Christ, God incarnate. John the Evangelist says, *"No one has ever seen God, but God the One and Only, who is at the Father's side, has made him known"* (v. 18). Jesus himself said, "No one has seen the Father except the one who is from God" (John 6:46), and, "Anyone who has seen me has seen the Father" (John 14:9). The apostle Paul told us, "For God, who said, 'Let light shine out of darkness,' made his light shine in our hearts to give us the light of the knowledge of the glory of God in the face of Christ" (2 Cor. 4:6). Jesus is the fulfillment of Isaiah's prophecy: "To us a child is born, to us a son is given" (Isa. 9:6). He is Immanuel, God with us. And because Jesus Christ has revealed God to us, we are blessed.

J. I. Packer correctly says that the greatest mystery of the Christian faith is not the resurrection of Christ or his miracles, but his blessed incarnation: "the plurality of persons in the unity of God, and the union of Godhead and manhood in the person of Jesus." Packer further states, "Once the Incarnation is grasped as a reality . . . other difficulties will dissolve."[22] Let us, then, examine this Word made flesh.

The Eternal Word

In the prologue of his gospel, John declares several truths about the Logos, the eternal Word:

"In the beginning was the Word" (v. 1). According to the Old Testament, the Word was God's self-expression and the agent of creation, revelation, salvation, and judgment. The psalmist says, "By the word of the LORD were the heavens made, their starry hosts by the breath of his mouth" (Ps. 33:6). Genesis 1:3 tells us, "God said, 'Let there be light,' and there was light." And in Psalm 107:20 we read, "He sent forth his word and healed them."

The Jewish people understood the Word as God's personal agent, while the Greeks such as Heraclitus thought of the Logos as the mind of God, the controlling principle that gives order to this world and to all men. John also points out that the Word had no beginning, but existed from eternity.

We reveal ourselves to others through our words, and God revealed himself to his creation through the personal agency of his eternal Word. God is not aloof and indifferent; in fact, he takes great delight in revealing himself to us.

"The Word was with God" (v. 1). In this simple phrase, John describes the personality of the Word, the Word's distinction from the Father, and the Word's close association with the Father. The Word has existed from all eternity as a distinct Person who partakes of the very essence of God and exists in eternal, intimate fellowship with him. Verse 18 says he is *"at the Father's side."* Thus, the incarnate Jesus prayed before he went to the cross, "Father, glorify me in your presence with the glory I had with you before the world began" (John 17:5).

"The Word was God" (v. 1). The Word was not just divine; John declares the Word was Deity. Many scriptures tell us that Jesus

---

22   J. I. Packer, *Knowing God* (Downers Grove, IL: InterVarsity, 1993), 53–54.

Christ is God himself. For instance, in verse 18 he is called "*God the One and Only*," and in John 20:28 Thomas declared, "My Lord and my God!" In Colossians 2:9 Paul writes, "For in Christ all the fullness of the Deity lives in bodily form."

The helpless infant born in a manger in Bethlehem is Deity wrapped in human flesh. Before John the Baptist was, before Isaiah was, before Abraham was, Jesus existed eternally. He is not a mere creature, despite what Arius of old and the Jehovah's Witnesses of today assert. John is saying that Jesus is God himself. This was a staggering statement for John, a strong, monotheistic Jew, to make. Yet he boldly affirms the deity of Christ.

The Word is God even as God the Father is God. Thus, the words and deeds of Jesus are those of God himself; to see Jesus is to see the invisible God. That is why we must repent of our sins and love, trust, and worship Jesus, who is God with us.

"*Through him all things were made*" (v. 3). The Father created all things visible and invisible, in heaven and on earth, through the personal agency of the Word, and "*without him nothing was made that has been made*" (v. 3; see also Col. 1:16–17). He is not part of creation; rather, all things were created by him and for him, and all things hold together because of him. He sustains all creation, including wicked beings, and is heir of all things (Heb. 1:2).

Romans 1:20 tells us that creation reveals God's invisible qualities of omnipotence and divine nature. All creation is due to the direct action of God the Word, not of some inferior divine emanation. The Word created the world *ex nihilo*. Thus, matter is not essentially evil, nor is creation eternal; all creation depends on Christ for its existence and sustenance.

"*In him was life*" (v. 4). The true origin of all physical life is not in chemicals, but in Christ. He is life, and he gives life to creation; therefore, we have DNA and RNA digital codes. There is intelligent design to the universe, and from this gospel we understand that the Designer is none other than Jesus Christ, the eternal Word.

Not only is Christ the source of physical life, but he is also the source of spiritual life. Jesus declared that he has life in himself even as the Father has life in himself (John 5:26). Jesus also said, "I am the resurrection and the life" (John 11:25). Jesus came to give us abundant, eternal life; no one else can do so.

"That life was the light of men" (v. 4). The Word gives indirect light to every man through creation (Rom. 1:18–20) and through conscience. He gives direct light to us through the sacred Scriptures, and personal light through his incarnational life. What is that light? It is the revelation of who God is, who man is, what atonement, hell, and heaven are, and what is the way of salvation.

There is no light apart from the eternal Word, for all truth radiates from Christ. All science—indeed, all knowledge—is possible only because of Christ. He is light and he enlightens everyone; therefore, we are all without excuse.

John says this light shines continuously in the darkness of this morally wicked world, but the darkness has not overcome it (v. 5). In John 3:19, he elaborates: "Light has come into the world, but men loved darkness instead of light because their deeds were evil." In 2 Corinthians 4:4, Paul also explains, "The god of this age has blinded the minds of unbelievers, so that they cannot see the light of the gospel of the glory of Christ, who is the image of God." But then he adds, "For God, who said, 'Let light shine out of darkness,' made his light shine in our hearts to give us the light of the knowledge of the glory of God in the face of Christ" (2 Cor. 4:6). The true light, the ultimate revelation of God, has come to us in Jesus Christ; we must either receive this light or reject it.

The Word Became Flesh

God finally revealed himself to us in Jesus Christ, God incarnate. Verse 14 tells us, *"The Word became flesh."* Notice, John does not say, "He became man," or "He took on a body." Rather, he uses blunt language to deal with the Docetic heresy of that time. The Docetists believed that all matter was evil and that God, therefore, could not come into contact with physical flesh. According to them, Jesus only appeared to be human, but he was not, in reality, true man.

But John emphatically declares, *"The Word became flesh."* The baby in the manger was God incarnate. The only begotten eternal Son of God became a helpless baby in Mary's womb and was born in need of Mary's loving care. Although he had to grow up and learn, he did not cease to be Deity. He took upon himself human nature and was subject to temptation, yet was without sin.

The Chalcedonian Creed describes him thus:

> Begotten before all ages of the Father according to the Godhead, and in these latter days, for us and for our salvation, born of the Virgin Mary, the Mother of God, according to the Manhood; one and the same Christ, Son, Lord, Only-begotten, to be acknowledged in two natures, inconfusedly, unchangeably, indivisibly, inseparably; the distinction of natures being by no means taken away by the union, but rather the property of each nature being preserved, and concurring in one Person and one Subsistence, not parted or divided into two persons, but one and the same Son, and only begotten, God the Word, the Lord Jesus Christ, as the prophets from the beginning have declared concerning him, and the Lord Jesus Christ himself has taught us, and the Creed of the holy Fathers has handed down to us.[23]

The enfleshed Jesus was born in Bethlehem for the sole purpose of going to Calvary to suffer and die. Why was this necessary? Because all have sinned and fall short of the glory of God (Rom. 3:23), and because the wages of sin is death (Rom. 6:23). No sinful man can pay the penalty for his sin and redeem himself (Ps. 49:8–9). Unregenerate man cannot perfectly obey God's law, so God himself became man in Jesus Christ. He became our representative, substitute, and mediator, that he might fully obey God's law by his life and death.

Hebrews 2:14–15 speaks about this enfleshment of the Word: "Since the children have flesh and blood, he too shared in their humanity so that by his death he might destroy him who holds the power of death—that is, the devil—and free those who all their lives were held in slavery by their fear of death." By his death, Jesus destroyed death for us and granted us life everlasting. And he did so willingly. When he came into the world, he said: "Sacrifice and offering you did not desire, but a body you prepared for me; with burnt offerings and sin offerings you were not pleased. Then I said, 'Here I am—it is written about me in the scroll—I have come to do your will, O God'" (Heb. 10:5–7). It was the will of God that Jesus die the death of a criminal on the cross for our salvation, and he embraced that will.

---

23 Wayne Grudem, *Systematic Theology* (Grand Rapids: Zondervan, 1994), 1169–1170.

What was the purpose of Christ's incarnation? The Word became flesh that he might offer himself as the only sufficient, acceptable, perfect sacrifice for our sins. Jesus Christ "was delivered over to death for our sins and was raised to life for our justification" (Rom. 4:25). "He is the atoning sacrifice for our sins, and not only for ours but also for the sins of the whole world" (1 John 2:2). John tells us, "God so loved the world that he gave his one and only Son, that whoever believes in him shall not perish but have eternal life" (John 3:16). John also writes, "This is love: not that we loved God, but that he loved us and sent his Son as an atoning sacrifice for our sins" (1 John 4:10).

We Received Grace

In the fullness of time, the Word became flesh. He came from heaven into the world that he created, but his world did not recognize him, love him, believe in him, submit to him, or worship him. Instead, it rejected him. Even his own people, the nation of Israel, did not welcome him, but called him a Samaritan, a drunkard, an illegitimate son, Beelzebub, and a blasphemer. They arrested him and handed him over to the Gentiles to be crucified.

Yet that was not the whole story. If it were, the incarnation would have been a defeat and God would have failed in his attempt to save his people. No, the incarnation was a success, for the moral darkness of the world could not overcome the light of Christ. Although the vast majority of people hated him, yet there were some who loved him and were saved by him. We read about such people in verse 12: *"Yet to all who received him . . ."* These welcomed Jesus as the God/man, the Savior and Redeemer, the one in whom there is life, light, and atonement for sin. Hearing of him and believing in him, they confessed and repented of their sins, and entrusted themselves to him. They called him "Lord and God" and became his disciples and witnesses. Some even died for their faith, such as Stephen, James, Peter, Paul, and many others throughout the history of the church.

Verse 12 says that those who so believed were given *"the right to become children of God."* As such, they enjoyed salvation and full fellowship with God. As God's children and heirs, they were protected, provided for, guided, and kept. These people were *"born of God"* (v. 13). Natural descent, human decision, desire of the husband—all these mean nothing. What matters is whether we experience the miracle of new birth, in which God places his divine life in our soul. We must ask whether we ourselves have experienced this divine, supernatural, mysterious, unilateral work of God.

Those who beheld God's glory as he tabernacled among men in human flesh (v. 14) were seeing with their physical eyes God's glory in the face of Jesus Christ. They saw it in his words and in his deeds, in his transfiguration, in his sufferings, in his resurrection, and in his ascension. John says, *"No one has ever seen God, but God the One and Only, who is at the Father's side, has made him known"* (v. 18). The phrase *"made him known"* comes from the Greek verb from which we get our words "exegesis" and "exegete."

How many people see nothing unusual in Jesus! But the elect of God see him as the explainer and revealer of the invisible God. He is uniquely qualified to do so because he has been eternally with God the Father. John tells us that the Word who was at the Father's side has revealed the Father to us. So we know the Father through the Son. Through Jesus, we realize that the Father loved us enough to send his one and only Son to die that he might give us life. Through Jesus, we realize that the Father is compassionate, gracious, and eager to forgive our sins.

Verse 14 says Jesus Christ is *"full of grace and truth,"* and verse 16 tells us, *"From the fullness of his grace we have all received one blessing after another."* What is grace? Unmerited favor. We who believe in Jesus receive from him grace upon grace. We receive grace to believe and grace to live every moment of our lives, both now and forevermore.

We all need grace. Through grace we receive life, though we merited death. Through grace we receive heaven, though we merited hell. Through grace we receive justification, though we merited condemnation. Through grace we receive reconciliation, though we merited estrangement. Because the Word became flesh, we receive what we really need. God himself tells us, "My grace is sufficient for you" (2 Cor. 12:9).

In 2 Corinthians 8:9, Paul makes this profound statement: "For you know the grace of our Lord Jesus Christ, that though he was rich"—meaning he was eternally God—"yet for your sakes he became poor"—referring to his incarnational life—"so that you through his poverty might become rich." We are made rich by the grace that flows to us abundantly through Jesus Christ. In 2 Corinthians 9:8 we read, "And God is able to make all grace abound to you, so that in all things at all times, having all that you need, you will abound in every good work." This is the purpose of grace.

In Revelation 3:14–22, the Laodicean church is described as "wretched, pitiful, poor, blind and naked," yet they pretended to have need of nothing. But the glorified Christ told them, "Here I am! I stand at the door and knock. You are poor, blind, and pitiable. But I have everything that you need: I offer you grace!" Of his fullness we have received one grace after another. Wave after wave of sufficient grace comes to us in Jesus Christ.

What about You?

God in Jesus Christ desires to be present in our lives to forgive our sins, bless us with eternal life, and guide us to heaven. We are poor sinners, but he became poor that we might become rich through his poverty. Yes, the world did not recognize him, and his own people did not believe in him. But that is not the whole story. Some did recognize him, believe in him, love him, and worship him.

What about you? Have you seen his glory? Have you believed in him and received him as your Lord and Savior? Have you received the grace that he brings? The word "grace" is related to the word "joy," for grace causes us to rejoice, even in tribulations. I pray that you will believe in Jesus Christ, the Logos, the eternal Word, and receive him today, that he may bestow on you his all-sufficient grace and eternal life.

Grace and Glory Ministries

GRACE & GLORY
MINISTRIES

Grace and Glory Ministries is an extension of Grace Valley Christian Center. We are committed to the teaching of God's infallible word. It is our mission to proclaim the whole gospel to the whole world for the building up of the whole body of Christ.

For more information about Grace Valley Christian Center, or to obtain additional copies of this book, visit www.gracevalley.org.